Thomas Clarke

The Battle and other Poems

Patriotic and Humorous

Thomas Clarke

The Battle and other Poems
Patriotic and Humorous

ISBN/EAN: 9783337306915

Printed in Europe, USA, Canada, Australia, Japan

Cover: Foto ©Thomas Meinert / pixelio.de

More available books at **www.hansebooks.com**

ATTLE,

R POEMS,

ꙮumorous;

E,

in May," etc.

CLARKE & CO

DARVEAU & CLARKE, PRINTERS,

170 Washington St., Chicago.

CONTENTS.

PREFACE.

It is proper to inform the reader, that many of the poems in this volume, especially those written during the rebellion, have already been published in various papers; and, it is hoped, have exerted some influence on the public mind, for the good of the country. Although deeply tinged with the feelings, perhaps with the prejudices of the times in which they were written, they will yet serve to throw a light on the history of that period, which could not be derived from any other source. A few of the pieces in this collection might justly lay claim to something of a prophetic character, if the author were disposed to affect the marvellous or the supernatural. He merely states this to illustrate a truth established of old, that

> "Great experience may attain
> To something of prophetic strain,"

and that a careful observer of passing events can hardly fail to be impressed with the coming issues, if he will view them by the unerring light of the past.

To illustrate : — The poem entitled "The Praise of Liberty" was printed, as it now stands, in the Springfield (Ill.,) Register, in the year 1856.

"The Ode for the New Year, 1858," was printed in the Springfield (Ill.,) Journal, on January 1st of that year, as it is given in this book. It will be seen at a glance, that the prophecy it contains has been verified to the letter.

"The Ode for the New Year, 1862," published in the Union Herald, of Springfield, (Ill.,) contains a prophecy respecting Great Britain, which is even now on the eve of accomplishment; and which the present generation will doubtless see fulfilled. Other examples might be given, did space permit.

With regard to the poems of the Revolution, contained in this collection, the reader will find the author's views more fully explained in the following INTRODUCTION.

INTRODUCTION.

"Brave men lived before Agamemnon," says Horace; "but the glory of their achievements died with them, because they lacked the sacred poet to hand down their fame to posterity." The "sacred poet" here indicated was Homer.

Homer! The very name is fraught with associations of grandeur, sublimity, heroism and all that is great and glorious amongst men; and the noble strains he has sung will live as long as this earth shall endure.

But his theme is not adequate to the strain; the workmanship surpasses the material; and the poet has far more honor from the manner in which he treats his subjects, than the heroes themselves, whose deeds, though for the most part meritorious, have been ren-

dered still more illustrious by the splendor imparted
to them through the medium of the poet.

The theme of the Iliad is the wrath of a single
hero and the siege and capture of a single city by
associated Greece, to avenge the private wrongs of a
prince whose cause they had sworn to defend; and
on this slight foundation has been built the most
noble poetical structure, the grandest monument of
human genius that has ever been created by man, and
bequeathed to a grateful posterity for its delight and
instruction.

We are at a loss to imagine what might have been
the nature of that poet's song, if he could have had
such a theme for his muse as the great American
Revolution; if, instead of the wrath of one man, his
theme had embraced the wrath of millions; if, instead
of the siege of a single city, he had had to describe
the invasion of a mighty continent; and if, instead of
the private wrongs of a single prince, he had been
forced to depict the intolerable wrongs of a whole
nation — the wrongs of humanity embodied in that

nation — who can conceive what might have been the grandeur of his strain and the mighty thunders of his denunciation ?

It is but once in many generations that such a benefactor of the human race appears amongst men, and when he does appear, he is generally far in advance of his age, and is either unknown or unappreciated by his fellow men. This was the case with Homer.

By his own generation he was not recognized as that mighty monarch of poets which the world afterwards unanimously acknowledged him to be.

It was not until the eighth century before the Christian era, when Pisistratus had collected the poems of Homer into one volume, that his great merits, his extraordinary genius, began to be seen and felt by his countrymen.

But it may be said that had Homer lived in this age of universal literature, science and progress, his fate would have been different. He would at once have taken his proper position in society and been honored and rewarded according to his merits.

Perhaps so! Of one thing, however, there is no doubt. He would have had a far more noble theme for the exercise of his great powers than any presented to him in his own day. The American Revolution would have found in him an adequate exponent of its mighty principles, and its Agamemnon, the illustrious Washington, would not have been deprived of the "sacred poet" to do justice to merits which require a character similar to his for dignity and simplicity to duly appreciate, and a genius equal to his own to paint worthily.

That great revolution and its heroes still lack the "sacred poet" to hand down their glory and their fame to the most distant posterity. History alone cannot do this; for, at best, it is tame and inadequate to produce that vivid impression on the mind which is essential to the eternalizing of true fame.

It is the poet alone who can do justice in this department. Achilles and Agamemnon require their Homer; but where shall we find him?

Ages may pass away before such a consummation can be realized. But the time will come, at last.

Then, and not till then, will the great temple of our liberties be crowned with honor and glory.

In the meantime, we should each contribute our quota of labor to build up the contemplated structure. Some can work in the quarry, and some can hew out the marble; some can clear away the rubbish, and others prepare the foundation; all can and ought to work together, at least to provide the material and have it ready for the great architect when he shall appear.

The late rebellion, also, and the sacrifices and heroic deeds which have been exhibited, in order to quell the same, present scenes and incidents worthy of the grandest efforts of the muse; and are suggestive of themes which, if treated as they deserve, will conduce to the same glorious results.

With this object in view, the author of the present work has prepared a few corner stones which, perhaps, may be deemed worthy of a place in this great temple.

He wished also to keep alive in the bosoms of the present generation that appreciation and earnest love of liberty, for which their fathers have sacrificed so much; since in the enjoyment of peace and the other blessings of Heaven, men are too prone to forget their duties, and to become apathetic and careless in the performance of the same. The author, moreover, believed that the down-trodden nations of the old world might learn, from the example of American heroes, not only to value liberty in the abstract, but to risk their fortunes, lives and sacred honor to attain it.

For this end, he has embodied the most interesting portions of the revolutionary history, as well as of the late rebellion, in poetical pictures that, being condensed, they may impress the imagination more vividly, and thus be fixed indelibly on the memory.

And first and pre-eminent amongst all others, is that crowning glory of heroic patriotism and genuine manhood — the most stupendous event that ever occurred in any land — and that is the battle of Bunker Hill. No battle of ancient or modern times can be compared with this in moral grandeur and the mighty results which sprung from it.

Marathon, Thermopylæ, Salamis and Platæa were insignificant, when compared with Bunker Hill, both in the circumstances that surrounded them and the events which followed. Even the most bloody and obstinate conflicts of the late rebellion, though on a far more extensive scale, fall infinitely short of Bunker Hill in one essential point. All these struggles were carried on by disciplined troops brought face to face with disciplined troops, whatever might be their disparity in numbers and strength; but Bunker Hill was the victory of the people over the tyranny of despotism. It presented the sublime spectacle of a people without skilled leaders, without discipline, without arms and ammunition, rising up in their majesty and defying the serried ranks of a mighty empire — troops accustomed to battle and flushed with victory, conscious of their strength, and marching with drums beating and colors flying, as if to certain victory — as if they were about to swallow up the small band of simple rustics who awaited their attack in perfect silence, as though awe-struck by the display of so much pomp, so much noise and so much valor; but who, to the astonishment of their assailants, still remained steadily at their posts, behind the frail entrenchments they had hastily thrown up in the night, until they could distinctly discern the "white" of an enemy's eye; and then, instead of slinking off in affright, they received the exulting foe with such a welcome of bullets, with such volleys of musketry admirably directed and perseveringly sustained, as to cause them to pause in their career for a moment, and then suddenly break their ranks and fly, in order to escape the inevitable death which stared them in the face!

Rallied with difficulty by their officers and by cries of shame and threats of vengeance, they returned once and again to the attack, with the same fatal result. But the colonists lost the victory which they had already grasped, by a lack of arms and ammunition, supplied with which, their success had been secured. Even their repulse was equal to a victory; for not only did it teach the colonists their own strength, but it showed the British tyrants what sort of enemies they had to contend with, and it so damped their courage, that it may truly be said to have been the hinge upon which the ultimate success of the American cause turned. Hence it is the noblest theme of this nature which could possibly be chosen to celebrate the force of character, the tenacity of purpose, the patriotism and the heroic courage of any people; and the wonder is, that it has not long since been seized upon by some of the eminent American poets who have adorned the literature of their country with the productions of their genius.

It has been the aim of the author to paint the absorbing events and stirring scenes of this great battle in their simple and natural colors, so as to give the reader a view of it as it was, and thus fix its scenes, as well as the principles which gave them being, indelibly on his mind.

In the following poem, the narrative is supposed to proceed from one who took an active part in the whole affair, and who, therefore, could be supposed to give a true and vivid idea, not only of the external scene, but also of the feelings, the hopes and fears of those who took a part in it as actors, and those who were merely spectators.

Here it will be seen that poetry takes a higher stand-point than history; for while the latter is a calm and unimpassioned narrative of events as they occurred in the past, it is the province of the former to reproduce the past with all its scenes and feelings, and to present them to our view as if they were transpiring before us; thus enlisting all our sympathies in the events, and causing us to take sides with the actors, whether we will or no.

Such have been the views and aims of the present writer. How far he may have succeeded in realizing them, it is not his to judge. It is for the candid reader to judge this matter and decide for himself.

THE BATTLE OF BUNKER HILL.

Entrenched on Bunker Hill we stood,
  A patriotic band,
(Excuse the boast,) prepared to die
  Or free our fatherland.
And we had labored all night long
  To raise the rampart high,
Nor ceased our toil when morning's beam
  Had tinged the Eastern sky.
Now by that dubious, twilight ray
  We scanned the scene around;
The neighboring city in the shade
  Was wrapped in sleep profound;

Save that when dreams of pending ill
  Disturbed the sleepers' sleep,
As some would turn upon their couch,
  Or wake to sigh and weep;
For hostile troops, the livelong night,
  Were pacing to and fro;
And sentinels exchange the word,
  As to their posts they go.
And oft an oath or drunken brawl
  Would strike the slumberer's ear,
Whom turning to his couch once more,
  A pleasing thought would cheer.
For well he knew, beyond the walls
  A host of heroes lay,
Prepared to march at Freedom's call,
  And sweep the foe away.

Beneath the hill on which we stood
  A peaceful village slept,
Which soon might be a ruined mass,
  From its foundation swept:

The distant bay to eastward stretched,
  Unruffled by a breeze ;
The tranquil river lay beneath ;
  Around were flowers and trees,
Whence little warblers poured their lays,
  Unconscious of all ill ;
The cock's shrill clarion sounded clear
  O'er rock and dale and hill ;
The cattle, as they hied to field,
  With lowings filled the air ;
All nature, save the heart of man,
  Seemed void of fear or care ;
But he dejected and forlorn
  Is prone to doubt and fear,
When dangers press, till gleams from heaven
  His drooping spirits cheer ;
Then trusting to this tower of strength
  From which his course to scan,
He soars above the ills of life,
  And feels himself a man.
Such sentiments our souls inspired,
  As there we stood and thought

That freedom for our fatherland
  Might by our hands be wrought;
That haply, too, the sacred spot
  On which we raised that mound
Might, in the future pilgrim's eyes,
  Be consecrated ground;
That distant lands and ages might
  Our love and valor praise,
And columns to our glorious deeds
  In grateful memory raise.
But hark!   The Lively, British sloop,
  Our strong position spies,
And, to dislodge us from the post,
  By cannonading tries.
But vainly on our ramparts firm
  Her shells and bullets fall;
One only man is hurt; the rest
  Work steady on the wall;
Until our stakes are deeply set,
  Our cross-ties well knit in,
And we are ready for the fight;
  So let the fight begin!

Meanwhile, the steeples, roofs and heights
  Of Boston and all round,
With anxious, palpitating hearts,
  To view the fight, were crowned.
What strange emotions filled men's souls,
  As there they gazing stood!
Two daring hosts prepared to shed
  Each other's kindred blood!
One gleaming bright in shining steel,
  Backed by an empire's might;
The other having no prestige
  Save courage based on right;
Ill clothed, worse armed, undisciplined,
  Discouraged by the ban
Through which base tyranny unnerves
  The arm — blots out the man;
And risking, by a single cast,
  Their country, honor, fame;
One doubtful hour must now decide
  The slave's or hero's name!
Good Heavens! it is a fearful risk;
  To Heaven they bend in prayer;

" God for the right incline the fight!"
   And hope succeeds to fear.

Soon from our ramparts we descried
   The British force advance,
A gallant host as ever bore
   A banner, sword or lance;
Bright glanced their armor in the sun;
   Bright gleamed their scarlet sheen;
Proud was their tread and confident;
   Their courage bold and keen.
Their flag waved lightly in the breeze;
   Loud pealed their trumpet's clang,
But to its threatening voice the rocks
   Alone responsive rang!
The infantry upon their right
   By gallant Howe were led;
Upon their left the grenadiers
   Bold Pigot marshalled;
Their numbers were two thousand strong,
   All veterans well tried,

While fifteen hundred raw recruits
We mustered on our side.

And now the cannon's opening roar
Announced their work begun;
But oft they paused in their career
To view the mischief done.
Meantime, behind our ramparts, we,
Unmoved, reserved our fire,
Until the British line advance
Yet nigher still and nigher.
"Brothers," brave Warren cried, "be men!
God will confound the wrong,
The race is not unto the swift,
The battle to the strong!
Remember, on each arm, this day,
Not merely hang your lives;
You fight for homes and altars free,
For sweethearts and for wives.
The insolent foe advance with pomp
Your courage to alarm;

Teach them the mighty power that sleeps
　　Within a yeoman's arm!
That patriots in their country's cause
　　Are towers of strength, and still
Can crush tyrannic power sustained
　　By mercenary skill!
Be cool — when of the foemen's eyes
　　The whites you can descry,
Take steady aim, each bullet then
　　Full fledged with death shall fly.
But see, they come!   Make ready, boys,
　　Present, now FIRE!" — A roar
Of muskets booms; our trenches blaze!
　　Incessant volleys pour　　　　　　.
A storm of death and ruin wild
　　Amongst the British ranks;
They pause, they falter, see! they break
　　In centre and both flanks,
And now, they rush confused, pell mell,
　　Down toward the landing place!
Oh, had you heard our joyous cheers
　　As we beheld that race!

And had you seen the battle ground,
  As dust and smoke gave way;
There many a gallant British heart
  Or dead or wounded lay!
Alas! it is a fearful sight,
  To view the silent dead,
Far from their homes and native skies,
  Stretched on their gory bed!
What tender ties, what fervid hopes,
  Are rent and blasted here!
What tortures must their fate inflict
  On distant loved ones dear!
Yes, fearful are the pangs that rend
  The tortured soldier's heart,
Far from his country doomed to die,
  From loved ones far apart!
No friendly hand to give relief
  Or staunch the streams that flow
From mortal wounds, or soothe the grief
  The world can never know!
Oh war! thou art a fearful scourge,
  And only justified

When for our liberties and life
  We call thee to our side.
But rest the blame where blame is due;
  Yea, on yon tyrant band,
That would invoke thee without cause,
  To desolate our land !

But see! they rally on the plain;
  Will they the fight renew ?
They come! but slower is their march,
  More circumspect their view;
And when, at length, with cautious tread,
  They ventured full in sight,
Our little band was well prepared
  To re-commence the fight.
"My gallant hearts," brave Prescott cries,
  "Receive them as before!"
'T is done! and lo! their foremost ranks
  Lie weltering in their gore!
As the wild wave breaks on the beach,
  And sadly sobbing dies,

So the brave, living wave of men
  Falls prone no more to rise!
As the tall poppies in the field
  Are swept by the mower's might,
So the fair forms, in bloom of youth,
  Death swallows from the light!
Or, as th' autumnal prairie grass
  Is melted by the blaze,
The bristling field of armed men
  Is melted from our gaze!
But, as on ocean's restless breast
  Fresh wave to wave succeeds,
Untiring valor still supplies
  The vacant place, and bleeds;
Till galled, at length, they halt, they break,
  And hark! that bugle's clang!
In full retreat they fly confused,
  And stung with many a pang!
'T is hoped these braves have had enough;
  Cheer, boys! the fight is won!
Another cheer! Kind Heaven will bless
  The work this day begun!

Each hero grasped his comrade's hand,
  And thus unto him spoke:

"Brother, this day our land is free
  From slavery's galling yoke!
I bless the day, I bless the hour,
  When first I saw the light!
I bless the glorious privilege
  Of mingling in this fight!
That here I stand before high Heaven,
  And feel th' ecstatic glow,
The boundless raptures of delight
  Which none but freemen know!
We've learnt our strength; our cause is won;
  For never more again
Can he who feels the freeman's glow
  Be bound by tyrant's chain!
The slave may bend his neck and live,
  And crawl — but as for me,
May death that instant break my bonds
  When cease I to be free!"

But Clinton from the Battery
   On Copp's Hill viewed this scene —
His veterans' defeat and shame —
   And writhed with anguish keen.
Full quickly passed he o'er the strait,
   And 'midst his soldiers stood.
" Oh, shame upon you!" he exclaimed,
   In fierce and threatening mood,
" What! shall old England hear it said
   That her best veterans fly,
Like sheep, before a rebel horde?
   No, let us rather die!
Wheel, wheel! myself shall lead you on
   To victory or death!"
A cheer was raised; while quick his sword
   He drew from out its sheath.

On, on they rush with hasty tread,
   And vengeance in their eyes;
And fierce to their defiant cheers
   Our musketry replies.

Dread was the conflict now, and blood
  Like streams of water ran;
Our men took cool, deliberate aim,
  And each brought down his man.

Oh, he alone might paint that scene
  Who paints the earthquake's throes,
The mad tornado's frightful sweep,
  The lava as it flows!
The thundering guns; the whizzing balls;
  The combatants' fierce cheers;
The hand-grenades; the clash of swords;
  The gleam of pikes and spears;
The strong man's mad, convulsive grasp,
  Struck down in his career;
The dying soldier's hopeless look,
  The stamp of pain and fear;
The mangled limbs that lay all round;
  Dissevered heads whose eyes
Glared fierce in death; and headless trunks;
  And spouting arteries; —

Oh, God! this was a fearful sight!
　　Terrific were these sounds!
It seemed as if the infernal crew
　　Had overleapt their bounds,
And, bursting hell's domain, usurped,
　　With poison-freighted breath,
The forms of mortals, for a time,
　　And revelled but in death!

But still the British soldiers fought
　　Undaunted as before;
Although our practice thinned their ranks,
　　And hundreds bathed in gore.
Had not our ammunition failed,
　　Not one of all their crew
Had e'er returned across the sea
　　His native land to view.
But when they saw our slackening fire,
　　And understood the cause,
They rushed at once upon our works,
　　Nor longer stood to pause.

With muskets clubbed and rusty swords
  A while we them withstood;
Till we, at length, were forced to yield
  To their o'erwhelming flood.
With faces scowling on the foe
  We sullenly withdrew;
So hacked and shattered were their ranks
  They dared not us pursue;
For half their number, on the hill,
  Or dead or wounded lay;
And many a British child unborn
  Shall rue that fatal day!
And when the insolent foe shall slight
  Our courage or our skill,
Let this proud answer meet their jeers:
  "Remember Bunker Hill!"

EDMUND BURKE

IN PARLIAMENT REBUKES THE TORIES WHO DE-
FEATED HIS CONCILIATION BILL FOR THE
COLONIES.

So ye would have it! Be it so!
　Know ye what ye have done?
Chains have ye forged for your own limbs;
　Your tyrant race is run!
The sleeping lion ye have roused,
　The infant giant woke;
And soon you'll shrink in sore affright,
　Recoiling from his stroke.
I see, beyond the western wave,
　A mighty nation rise;
The nurse of freemen, whose fair fame
　Shall pierce the vaulted skies:
I see her sails fill every port;
　And, from these distant isles,
Her bosom opens to receive
　Those whom your fear exiles;

The good and true of every rank,
    Who scorn to bend the neck,
Or bow to idols raised by power,
    Obedient to your beck.
Who nobly spurn the ghostly chains
    Your bigots would impose;
Who trust to Heaven their rightful cause,
    And in its smile repose; —
These with an overwhelming wave
    Will sweep you out of sight;
And bury you and your pretense
    Deep in the gloom of night;
So deep, that when geologists
    Or antiquarians keen
Shall seek to find some traces left
    Of what you once had been;
Your disembowelled fossils long
    They 'll ponder o'er in vain;
But failing to trace your extinct race,
    Will hurl them back again.
The colonists, you say, must ask
    Your leave for breath to live!

And tax them as ye please, yet still
   They must not wince, but give!
Fools, idiots, puppies, popinjays!
   Where were ye, tell me, where,
When yonder hardy colonist
   Was struggling with the bear?
Or when the savage Indian band
   Beset his homeward way,
Where were ye then to grant him leave
   To keep the foe at bay?
I see you shrug your shoulders up,
   And fold your silken hand,
And proudly draw your ermine robe;
   Can ye not understand?
What! Hear ye not the rising storm?
   The rumbling thunder's groan?
The mighty wind's tempestuous howl?
   The ocean's sullen moan?
Enough! Whom Heaven would overwhelm,
   Heaven renders deaf and blind;
They drift, like wrecks without a helm,
   The sport of waves and wind.

WM. PITT, (LORD CHATHAM,)

IN REPLY TO THE TORIES' PROPOSITION INSISTING
THAT THE COLONISTS MUST ADMIT THE RIGHT
OF BRITAIN TO TAX THEM.

What novel scheme of tyranny
    Is this ye would propose?
Its whispers reached my sickly couch
    From which with pain I rose,
To lift my solemn warning voice
    Against the damning deed
By which ye doom so many men
    To suffer and to bleed!
For sake of justice, think in time,
    Pause in your mad career;
Nor let your reason yield the reins
    To passion and to fear.
The colonists ye mean to tax,
    Without their vote or will;

"They are our subjects," ye exclaim;
   "And we shall rule them still!"
As far as sovereign power extends,
   I grant the king has right
To exercise a just control,
   And rule, if forced, by might;
But taxes are a free-will gift;
   And tyranny alone
Can wring them from th' unwilling hand,
   By force of nerve and bone.
Besides, these are our countrymen,
   Our kindred flesh and blood;
And are their rights the less because
   They dwell beyond the flood?
Then unto them the golden rule
   Still practice and apply;
"Do unto others as ye would
   By others be done by."
Their strong resistance wakes your wrath,
   And with a husky voice,
You call them "rebels;" but for me,
   My lords, I must rejoice; —

Rejoice to think our noble race

    Are free, wherever found ;

And that no chains can e'er be forged

    Whereby they may be bound ;

'T were sad to see three millions dead

    To Freedom's sacred claim ;

Such apathy would stain our blood,

    Our Anglo-Saxon name.

Now, in a just an l noble cause,

    Our power might earth defy ;

But in this dark, unjust crusade,

    Our strength would wane and die ;

For though America should yield,

    Like Samson, she would fall

Grasping the pillars of the State,

    And thus o'erwhelm us all.

THE BEREAVED FATHER

BEWAILING HIS MURDERED CHILDREN AT WYOMING.

My children, oh! is this the end
 Of all my hopes and fears?
For this my days were spent in toil,
 My nights in sighs and tears?
For this I 've labored with my hands,
 And plodded with my head?
This harvest of my hopes I reap,
 My children, ye are dead!
Slain by the bloody hand of Brandt
 And his infernal crew;
Hounded on to this fell deed,
 John Butler, fiend, by you!
Their gaping wounds still pour out blood;
 With horror glare their eyes;
Revenge, oh God! give me revenge!
 Revenge! each rock replies!

Yes! by these precious life drops red,
  I swear to listening Heaven,
No quarter to the cruel foe
  By me shall e'er be given;
No joy, no comfort, shall I find
  In life's all-beauteous light,
Until John Butler's eyes are sealed
  In everlasting night.
And the fell crew, his satellites,
  With Brandt their chosen head,
Shall taste the bitter cup they gave,
  And mingle with the dead!

Oh, lovely vale of Wyoming!
  Where is thy beauty flown?
This blackened ruin, once my home,
  Is all I call my own!
But oh! my pearls of greatest price,
  My pretty prattlers, say,
Will you no more your father greet,
  At closing of the day,

With rapid, little twinkling feet,
   And smiles of infant joy;
And emulous climb on my knees,
   My darling girl and boy?
No more, no more! The worm instead
   Shall prey on each fair cheek;
And I heart-broken and forlorn,
   Shall death and danger seek,
Beneath yon glorious Stars and Stripes,
   And foremost in the fight,
I 'll glut my vengance on the foe,
   Then joyful quit the light.

.

THE LAMENT

My father and my mother with the hatchet they
    have slain,
And dragged their bodies through the streets—their
    tears and prayers were vain;
Like wild deer my fair sisters to their chambers
    they pursued,
And in their innocent, virgin blood their hands they
    have imbrued!
Oh, monsters! What could urge them thus to mur-
    der old and young?
They 've slain the mother with the babe that to her
    bosom clung!
They 've scattered death and ruin wild all o'er this
    lovely vale;
More devastating was their track than earthquake,
    flood or hail!

The Susquehanna flowing late with pure and tranquil
flood

Now winds its mournful course along tinged with its
children's blood.

Shall I stand here lamenting and inactive while the
cry

Of vengeance rises from this blood — re-echoed
from the sky?

Forbid it Heaven! My burdened heart shall quench
its grief and pain

In one o'erwhelming wave, revenge! — revenge for
martyrs slain!

WASHINGTON

RENOUNCING HIS ALLEGIANCE TO THE BRITISH —

ORIGIN OF AMERICAN EMBLEMS.

Oh, Britons, from your host of slaves
And subjects strike my name!
No more in your despotic ranks
I seek for wealth or fame.
I scorn your smiles — I dare your stripes,
Strip me of house and land!
Beneath yon starry roof of Heaven,
I then will take my stand.

Oh, happy thought! prophetic word!
Yes, from this very hour,
The STARS and STRIPES we will adopt,
As emblems of our power!
The stars to shield us, guide and cheer,
The stripes to gall our foes;
So that mankind this truth may learn;
FROM HEAVEN OUR HELP AROSE.

5

Sweet Freedom, weary, banished,
  I know not from what land,
Has lately sought a refuge here,
  On fair Potomac's strand:
There found we her in sorrow,
  And she seemed to know us well,
And oft would she point to our chains,
  And of our sufferings tell;
Till we, at length, began to feel
  The galling, bitter yoke,
And, rising irresistible,
  It from our necks we broke!
Then we beheld the Goddess fair
  In new-born beauty rise,
And stand in heavenly glory bright,
  Before our wondering eyes.
As when of old, at Marathon,
  Or sea-girt Salamis,
Before the Greeks she spread her flag,
  And cried: "Look but to this!"
So unto us with cheering voice,
  She cried: "Be worthy me,

And for all time to come, as now,
    Ye shall be blest and free;
Free as that glorious Spartan band
    At famed Thermopylæ ;
Free as in the beam of Heaven,
    Yon Eagle fans the sky !"

And as she spoke, the kingly bird
    From seaward hove in sight.
"Thus, thus," she cried, "doth Empire's power
    Still westward wing its flight;
This emblem, too, appropriate —
    Let this your banner be,
And still may Eagle, Stars and Stripes
    Float proudly o'er the free !"

MRS. MERRILL,

"What means that howling of the dogs?" said
　　Merrill to his wife;
"The Indians are upon us! we must fight for dearest
　　life."
Scarce had he uttered this, when hark! a shot is
　　fired outside;
A bullet aimed too well passed through and struck
　　him on the side.
"I'm wounded! oh, make fast the door!" he sank
　　as thus he spoke.
She seized an axe and closed the door which soon
　　the Indians broke;
Once in possession of the house, with tomahawk in
　　hand,
How could a lonely female then their fierce assaults
　　withstand?

In vain they tried to force their way, since, both in
    thought and deed,
That heroine could resources wield that served in
    time of need;
For she undaunted, though alone, their violence
    withstood,
And gave her thirsty axe to drink abundantly of
    blood.
Four of their number by her hand fell down to rise
    no more;
The door, the lintels and the walls were smeared
    with brains and gore.
Enraged and baffled in their aims, three mounted on
    the roof;
Two down the chimney would descend; the other
    stood aloof:
Just then, her only feather-bed she seized as quick
    as thought,
And on the embers flung the mass, which down the
    Indians brought,
Half suffocated by the smoke; and there they help-
    less lay,

Till by her axe they were dispatched on their
infernal way.

The last survivor with a sledge assailed the cabin
door;

A mighty blow that clove his cheek was followed by
a roar;

Then, reeling like a drunken man, beside the door
he fell:

Thus seven fierce imps by one weak hand were sent
express to hell!

And did she faint, and did she blanch, when she had
done the deed?

No! To her wounded husband next she turned her
care with speed;

Staunched his life's blood, recalled his strength, and,
with her soothing voice,

Revived his sinking spirits, while she caused him to
rejoice,

By pointing to the ghastly crew, all lifeless on the
ground:

"Thus perish all our Country's foes," she cried,
  "wherever found!"

Ye women of America, while virtue, valor, fame,
Are honored here upon our earth, forget not
  Merrill's name!

MISS McCREA,

MURDERED BY THE INDIANS.

"Oh, charming lily of the vale,
   Thy lover bids thee come;
Array thee in thy bridal robes,
   We come to bear thee home !"

"And who be ye that I should dress
   Obedient to your word ?"
"Oh, we are trusty Indian chiefs;
   This proof is from thy lord !"

They gave to her a written scroll,
   'T was in a well-known hand:
"Chiefs, I will dress and go with you
   Where'er ye may command !"

Soon from her chamber she came down
  Robed in her bridal sheen;
A lovelier form, a fairer face,
  No mortal e'er had seen!

Her kinsfolk all, with pride and love,
  Gazed on her peerless form;
The Indians' breasts with passion heaved,
  But soon they quelled the storm.

"Now, I am ready," she exclaimed
  "Dear friends, adieu, adieu!
The way is short, ere many moons
  I come to visit you."

Out spoke her tender mother first,
  While on her neck she hung;
"My daughter, oh, my eldest born,
  My heart with grief is wrung!

Wilt thou forsake thy childhood's home,
    The ties of kindred break,
And trust thyself with savage men,
    All for a stranger's sake?"

Her father grasped her by the hand,
    And tried to hide a tear;
"Wilt thou thy father leave forlorn,
    My child, my daughter dear?"

"This house will be a darksome wild,"
    Her little sister cried,
"When thou art gone, my sister dear;
    Then with us still abide."

Last came her brother; him she loved
    As dearly as her life;
"And wilt thou leave us, sister dear,
    To be a Briton's wife?

An English soldier bearing arms
   Against our country's cause !
No good can come of such a match ;
   My sister, turn and pause !"

But, disregarding all their prayers,
   Their sighs and scalding tears,
She yielded to the voice of love,
   Unmoved by doubts or fears.

She tore herself from their embrace,
   Nor longer would delay;
And drawing near the Indian chiefs,
   She bade them lead the way.

They led her over hill and dale,
   Through forest, glen and stream ;
And though the way was rough, yet hard
   To her it did not seem.

But now the chiefs, in loud debate,
   Their passions fierce disclose;
From angry words and angry looks
   They almost came to blows.

The subject of dispute was clear;
   The maiden was the cause;
With agonizing fears she heard
   Their threats — nor long they pause.

" Oh, Heaven !" she cried, " I see the glare
   Of murder in that eye !
My sands of life are near run out,
   And here I now must die !

My parents, sister, brother, friends,
   To you I bid farewell;
Too late my error I deplore ;
   My pangs no tongue can tell !

Oh, Britons, you I fondly loved,
   And for you would have died;
And for that soldier in your ranks
   Of whom I was the bride.

But now too late I see my crime,
   And blush for very shame,
That I should love my country's foe,
   Forget my country's fame!

Oh monsters! how could you let loose,
   With tomahawk and brand,
These fiends to shed your kindred blood
   And desolate the land?

Who spare nor age nor sex, but still
   Pursue, with keen delight,
The scent of blood, until the earth
   Is sickened at the sight.

Then cursed forever be the cause
  Which such fell means employs!
And triumph meet the cause that's just,
  In freedom's endless joys!"

'T was thus prophetic spoke the maid,
  Unblenched by fear of pain;
Assured that her dear fatherland,
  Ere long, would burst its chain!

THE OLD MAN ON THE CLIFF.

A PROPHECY.

I stood upon the lofty rock, deep under me the flood,

And let my spirit roam abroad in free and thoughtful
mood;

My vision ranged both far and wide, o'er land and
sky and sea,

No sound of bondage struck my ear, no traces could
I see.

The British flag no longer waved o'er mast, or hill,
or tower;

The glorious Stars and Stripes waved there, the
emblems of our power!

My swelling heart was raised to heaven in gratitude
and love,

And why, I cried, should paltry cares our inward
feelings move?

6

What private sorrows press the soul, let's drown
 them in the wave
Of pure delight that surges through the pulses of
 the brave!

I see a ship upon her course, her sails bedewed with
 spray;
Free prospering breezes waft her on and through
 her canvass play.
A happy voyage, sailors, all welcome and all hail!
Hail to your freight, hail to your ship, from keel to
 mast and sail!
Through the wild waves you steer your course; your
 port is right before;
Your banners bear the flowers of peace sprung from
 our heroes' gore!

It thunders in the distance — is it the sound of fight?
Or but the echoes of the waves that lash the shore
 with might?

My heart is stirred within me when I hear that
thunder tone,
But I 'm now too old for battle, yet, thank Heaven,
I have a son !

ADDRESS OF THE GREEKS

TO THE LOVERS OF THEIR ANTIQUITY AMONG THE
MODERN NATIONS OF EUROPE.

Much have ye written, sung and said, much envied
and bewailed,
Concerning our famed ancestors whose glory ye have
hailed;
And truly their great fame has passed along from
age to age,
To all the nations of the earth, and filled th' historic
page;
And he whose heart would glow for worth, for honor
or for fame,
Must from their slumbering ashes draw the sparks
that fan his flame.

Why, nations, why are ye so dumb, so sunk in apathy?
That spirit which ye have invoked, sprung from the
past, stands by!

And with a mingled look of pride and sorrow,
   points his hand —

To that famed spot, know ye it not? — the ancient
   Grecian land!

Those sparks concealed in ashes long wherein ye
   oft have sought,

That glow by which alone the soul true freedom has
   been taught;

Those latent sparks being duly fanned have burst
   into a blaze!

And yet ye stand inactive all, or shrink with wild
   amaze!

Oh shame upon you! is it thus ye trifle with their
   name?

Thus have your pointless darts been aimed, thus
   have ye prized their fame!

Too long you dallied with the theme, too much
   you 've said and sung,

Too far you 've wandered from the track; the old at
   length is young!

What heretofore ye distant deemed is now at length
    made near ;

It even now knocks at your gate, the sound can ye
    not hear ?

Its form appears before your eyes, robed in celestial
    light ;

Can ye not see it ? No, those orbs are dazzled by
    the sight !

One land there is beyond the flood and near the
    setting sun, —

That by Columbus won from night, redeemed by
    Washington ; —

That glorious land has caught a spark from Free-
    dom's funeral urn,

And kindled up a living flame which ne'er shall
    cease to burn.

Her stars and stripes proclaim her power o'er every
    land and sea ;

Ye nations, follow in her track, be daring and be
    FREE !

Rose-trees have I planted 'neath my window in the
    sun,

And they bloom and blossom sweetly, and into my
    chamber run;

And the little birds are singing joyful strains
    amongst their leaves.

Ye warblers, do ye stay to learn why my sad
    bosom grieves?

Ah! my lover is departed — gone to join the patriot
    band,

Who risk their lives and fortunes for our sacred
    fatherland;

Pray tell him not, ye warblers, that to staunch a
    hero's wound,

The silken scarf he gave me, from my neck I have
    unbound;

Nor that my golden ringlets sore neglected long
    have lain;

But tell him that my love for him must ever true
    remain!

Still linger on, ye warblers, till my lover fond return;

Bloom, bloom, ye lovely roses, till at length I cease
    to mourn;

And we, maidens, with the victors join in dance,
    and play, and song.

They come, oh joy! But where is he? In vain I
    search the throng!

Alas! where can I hide my head to shun the
    general joy?

One only warbler stays with me to mourn my
    warrior boy!

AN ODE FOR THE NEW YEAR. — 1858.

OLD YEAR.

Sweet sister mine, with tranquil eye,
  Thrice welcome from yon starry sphere!
Thrice welcome from thy throne on high,
  To watch and guard the rolling year!
The post I willingly resign,
  And, joyful, wing my flight once more,
By those bright beacon-lights that shine,
  To far Eternity's lone shore.

NEW YEAR.

Fair sister of the visage pale,
  O'er whose sad brow a cloud is hung,
Whose locks float loosely on the gale,
  Whose accents tremble on thy tongue,
Adown whose face the tear-drops flow,
  Oh, say, has sorrow plowed thy cheek?
Oh, say, is earth a scene of woe?
  In pity, gentle sister, speak!

OLD YEAR.

Not all! Take comfort; do not weep!
   Some green spots rise to cheer the sight,
Like islands from the oozy deep,
   Or stars that gem the brow of night.
I 've seen an Empire burst its chains;
   Yea, by an Autocrat's decree.
No Christian land, save one, remains
   By slavery cursed : all else are free.

But that exception! bitter thought!
   It makes my eye-balls swell with pain;
My inmost soul with grief is wrought,
   And tears flow down my cheeks like rain.
The land where LIBERTY was born
   And cradled, 'midst war's fearful strife,
That land its offspring hath forsworn,
   While CZARS and QUEENS protect her life!

How different from the days of yore,
   When mighty monarchs strove to crush

Her infant struggles in her gore —
  Her infant cries in death to hush!
A host of heroes, clad in mail,
  Like earth-born giants, sprang to life,
Placed wealth and honor in her scale,
  And armed themselves for mortal strife

Then WASHINGTON, the great and good,
  Unsheathed his sword in her defense;
Then HENRY poured th' o'erwhelming flood
  Of patriotic eloquence;
Then JEFFERSON's gigantic mind,
  Which grasped the great Creator's plan,
Proclaimed this truth for all mankind:
  MAN IS NOT BORN THE SLAVE OF MAN!

NEW YEAR.

'T is sad to think that truths so vast
Should now on barren sands be cast!

OLD YEAR.

Hope, sister!   My prophetic view
   Can, from the past, the future trace.
Taught by experience sad, yet true,
   I augur good for all the race.
Comes strife?   Then blood unjustly shed
   Shall vengeance claim, in thunder tones;
But Truth shall triumph; Justice spread
   On earth!   Or else, the very stones
Shall raise a wild, heaven-piercing cry,
   To plead for right and liberty!

ITEMS FROM PEKIN (ILL.)

MARCH, 1859.

Friend Brisque, you for items are evermore seeking,
And you ask me to send you some even from Pekin.
What! are they so scarce in the regions terrestrial
That you must have recourse to the empire
    celestial?
If so, I will aid you as far as I 'm able;
I have one or two waiting a chance on my table.
But, mum! lest the angels should punish me one
    day,
(And two, by the by, sat beside me last Sunday,)
For poaching the nectar ambrosial from Heaven;
If 't is known, I shall scarcely (I fear) be forgiven.

But now for the items for which you are itching;
You 'll find them most spicy — nay, almost be-
    witching.

I see you are smacking your lips! Not so hasty;
It is no bird's-nest soup, no, nor fat-puppy pasty;
No mess of lob-worms, no pot-de-rats stew,
But a delicate, well-seasoned mental ragout.

What! much disappointed! You thought it rich
    food
That was duly prepared by some Soyer or Ude.
Well, well, you're but mortal; I'd almost o'er-
    looked it,
Or else I'd have altered the dish ere I cooked it!

Once more for the items — To envy were sin;
For you know 'tis a Heaven here with us in Pekin.
Of hell we know nothing, except by conjecture,
Or hints from our eloquent Sawyer, by lecture;
It is true brother Rybolt creates a sensation,
At times, by a peep at the gulf of ———,
And snuffs up the air as if sulphur abounded;
And thus brother Loyd hath us sinners confounded.

But yet, we have much consolation withal;
Brother Chapin declares, hell is no where at all!
With this last decision I 'd fondly agree;
('T were a happy conclusion for you and for me;)
Had not our judge Harriot declared his opinion,
(And law o'er celestials still holds some dominion,)
" A hell may be useful, howe'er ye explain it;
A small one at least — we had better retain it."

" A small one!" quoth Haines: "If we keep one
    at all,
I very much fear that it cannot be small:
For, apart from your Rybolts, your Loyds and your
    Sawyers,
It must be of huge size, to make room for the
    lawyers!"

CELESTIALS IN CHICAGO;

OR, St. Peter on Stump-tail.

(A newly married couple, hailing from Pekin, (Ill.,) came to Chicago
to spend the honeymoon. What befel them, as related by the bride-
groom. TIME—When John, surnamed the Long, was Mayor of
Chicago.)

Of Chicago you wish me to give you my notion.
Well, friends, I comply; though with painful
    emotion.
Like Æneas relating to Dido his story,
With a sigh, I now lay my experience before you.

Chicago 's a place of a wonderful size;
When I saw it, my eyes, how I opened my eyes!
Such very big houses, big bugs and big women;
And a monstrous horse-pond for a body to swim in!

Astonished my wife gazed long time without
    speaking;
At length she exclaimed, "This is bigger than
    Pekin!
Good heart, what a city!" While thus we were
    glowering
Around us, with feelings alm·st overpowering
A chap, all politeness with bowing and scraping,
(If he was not a gentleman, sure he was aping,)
Came up, and said he, "You are strangers, I see;
I take such in always, then, pray, come with me!"

Well pleased with his manners, we followed his
    track;
While kindly he threw my big trunk on his back,
Which held all our money and clothing so pretty,
With which we hoped soon to astonish the city.

We thus jogged along, all unconscious of danger,
Till, at length, at a turn, we lost sight of the
    stranger:

Cried my wife, " Where 's the gentleman gone with
    the plunder ?"
Said I, " I should like to know that; and should
    wonder
If ever again we clap eyes on his features ;
These folks of Chicago are slippery creatures !"
And, truly, from that day to this we have sought him,
Through the city police, but have never yet caught
    him.
Can it be that one John, who is styled "Elongatus,"
Gives license to porters to rob people gratis?
" No, no !" you will say, while at this some may
    laugh,
" For John, though so long, is too honest by half !"

Chicago 's the place — I no longer can doubt it —
That St. Peter declared he knew nothing about it;
When a sinner who died there once knocked at
    Heaven's gate,
And the Saint thundered out, " Friend, I fear you 're
    too late;

Whence come you?   What are you, and what is
    your name?"

"I'm a porter by trade; from Chicago I came."

"Chicago! Chicago!" the Saint cried in doubt;
"If there is such a place I will ferret it out."
And he looked at the map: "Yes! yes! it is here,
A very large city; and yet, what is queer —
You are the FIRST soul that e'er ventured from thence
To trouble these regions!   Whence comes this, say,
    whence?"

"Look here!" said the porter, "my record's
    endorsed
By a champion who never yet has been unhorsed;
Who, mingling with Saints, is a Godly exhorter,
And the very best patron of porters and porter;
The 'broth of a boy,' whom all Paddies adore;
And they doubtless will send him to Congress once
    more;
A fit representative for such a city,
Who by turns can be jovial, or pious, or witty;

His name is LONG JOHN; he is down on stump-tail;
If that name has no weight here, sure nought can
   avail!"

"What! a pass from Long John, eh?" cried Peter,
   broad grinning;
"Go back whence you came; 'tis the Heaven
   you've been winning.
Stay there till you learn something better than this:
You are green if you know not the price of our
   bliss!
It is true that, of old, the poor here might find rest,
And the virtuous share in the joys of the blest.
Ah! then e'en the scrape of a pen from Long John
Would have taken ten souls, worse than thine, out
   of pawn;
But now 'tis TIN only that opens this gate;
Like old fashions, the virtues are here out of date.
Take a peep through this chink at our banqueting
   hall;
The keenest of shavers there lord it o'er all.

The men of your city draw fine on the strop ;

Your town is known here as 'the great shaving
  shop.'

Your preachers may prate about love there below ;

The love of the dollar is here ' all the go.'

Then, if you 'd partake of our bliss, ('t is no
  gammon,)

Bring a check for the gold on Emmanuel, from
  SCAMMON.'

"Oh, if that be the case," said our friend, with a
  smile,

"I, too, have shaved some, and have made up my pile,

By shaving from trunks, in the way of my trade ;

Although, to confess, I was sorely afraid ;

For, down in our town, we were constantly told,

That none could pass through your strait gate with
  his gold.

But they lied, I perceive, and rejoice it is so ;

Here 's a check for the gold ; 't is from Scammon
  and Co."

The Saint stood bewildered, delighted, amazed ;
While long on the porter in silence he gazed.
At length, he found breath, and accosted him thus :
"Are you sure, 'tis no joke that you put upon us ?"
"Cock sure !" said the porter, while Peter he eyed
With a look of insulted professional pride.

Then Peter exclaimed, over-brimming with joy ;
" By my soul, you 're a ' brick ;' you 're the ' broth of
    a boy ;'
A jolly good fellow !   But how did it come,
That you cheated the priests and the lawyers at
    home ?
Got away from their grasp with such treasure in
    store ?
Such a case, to my knowledge, ne'er happened
    before !"

" Oh ! of this," said the porter, " we 'll talk by
    and by,
O'er a good bowl of punch — smoking hot — of old
    rye :

8

At present, suffice it to say, all is right!

Let me pass to the music, the dance and the light,

Taking chance in the crowd if there turns up a
    fight!"

The Saint seized his hand and exclaimed, with a
    grin,

"I mistook you: excuse me! Dear friend, pray,
    walk in!"

THE PRAISE OF LIBERTY.

A VISION.

Written in 1856.

A baleful cloud o'erspread the skies of late,
Surcharged with sulphurous vapors — big with fate,
Which filled men's souls with horror and affright;
Freedom herself was sickened at the sight!

I saw the despots of the earth rejoice
Whilst forging chains.   I heard the bigot's voice
Exultingly exclaim : " Where now thy power,
Democracy?   Behold thy fated hour!
Thy votaries no more shall trust in thee ;
Slaves of a phantom, how can they be free?
Where now is Liberty, thy idol, flown ?
Go, seek her in the land of Washington!
Thy search how vain !"

The scene was palled in gloom,
And anarchy announced our country's doom;
Confusion reigned — the din of war arose,
And brothers stood opposed — most deadly foes;
Blood flowed in torrents; pestilence ensued;
And famine raged with all her horrid brood.
Still darker grew the storm, more fierce its roar,
Until its thunders swept from shore to shore.

At length, a gleam of light burst on my eyes;
The cloud had vanished from the smiling skies.
Fair Freedom showed once more her roseate face,
Where all her hopes and feelings I could trace.
Thy sun, oh Liberty, with radiance shone;
The tyrant trembled on his baseless throne.
Around, the landscape smiled in native green;
And joy illumined all the peaceful scene!

As young Alcides, in the dawn of life,
Slew two huge serpents sent by Jove's proud wife,

Jealous of the young hero's future fame;
So thou, fair Liberty, a nobler name,
Heaven-born like him, but of a destiny
More during and more glorious than he,
Hast slain two reptiles sent by foreign foes,
More envious of thy greatness and repose
Than Juno of the Theban Hercules,
REBELLION and DISUNION hight were these.

The monsters raised their slimy heads and crept
Around her chamber, while the Goddess slept,
Not dreaming that infernal fiends should dare
To breathe with her the same supernal air;
Filling the weak and timid with alarm,
They crawled about, in gloom, concocting harm,
And deeming the young damsel too supine
To crush their treason, though she were divine;
Till plumed by long impunity they spring
Sheer on her couch, each armed with deadly sting.

Their hissing roused the sleeper from her bed;
Her hireling menials, struck with terror, fled;

(Fit emblems of false friends, who slink away
When clouds obscure prosperity's fair day.)
Not so the heroine!   Up she quickly sprung,
Strong in her God-like nature, though so young;
The neck of either mischief prompt to clasp
She choked each struggling hydra in her grasp;
Unveiled the mystery of their horrid spell,
And drove the demons to their native hell!

Oh, noble, Godlike, sacred Liberty!
Whence shall I cull a chaplet worthy thee?
Thee from what treasures shall my spirit bless?
How my full heart its gratitude express?
Since thou hast crushed thy country's enemies,
All deem thee worthy of thy native skies;
The nations from afar shall sound thy fame;
And distant ages shall thy praise proclaim;
The oppressed in every clime shall raise their eyes,
Radiant with hope, to thy unclouded skies!
And souls that thirst for freedom long denied
Shall quaff thy streams and shall be satisfied!

Boldly hast thou proclaimed this glorious truth
Unfading as the Heavens' eternal youth;
That in America, the favored land
Of liberty, the despot shall not stand;
The bigot shall not plant the Upas tree;
That here — to worship God — the soul is free!
And that the common accident of birth
Must here give place to virtue and to worth.

Oh, ye who value Freedom's hallowed name,
Immunity from anarchy and shame,
Ye friends of order, wheresoe'er ye be,
Who prize "Unsullied homes and altars free;"
Who love to see fair commerce spread the sail;
And liberal arts o'er all the land prevail;
And peace and plenty reign with boundless sway;
Would ye enjoy these treasures,— then obey —
Obey the laws by which all-bounteous Heaven
The choicest blessings to this land hath given;
And rally now, with one accord, around
Yon glorious standard fixed in Freedom's ground.

Let North and South unite, with one acclaim,
To hail our standard-bearer's honored name;
And cry, from Maine to California's shore,
"The Union now — the Union evermore!"

THE FUGITIVE.

Inscribed to Owen Lovejoy, 1860.

.

Dark and drear was the night, saving when the red
   moon
Peeped at times through huge masses of laboring
   clouds;
But such moments were brief, for the heavens were
   soon
Enveloped once more in funereal shrouds.

And now from the regions around the bleak South,
Where night's gloomy curtain more darkly was
   thrown,
Streams of lightning in rapid succession burst forth,
And hollow the far distant thunder-clouds groan.

But quick and more quick gleams the lightning's red
 flash ;
And near and more near peals the thunder's loud
 roar ;
And hark ! 't is the thunderbolt's terrible crash,
And earth heaves and trembles from mountain to
 shore

As troubled my eye swept along the wild sky,
Wrought to madness extreme by the elements' strife,
Midst the hoarse peals of thunder I heard a weak
 cry
As of one who lamented the sorrows of life.

'T was a poor son of Africa, friendless, forlorn ;
The salt tears abundant his dark cheek bedewed ;
His locks in despair from his bare head were torn ;
And the ground all around with those drenched
 locks was strewed.

And he cried, " Oh, ye heavens enveloped in flame;
Ye clouds that your torrents pour down on my head;
Rage on in your fury!   Your pity I claim:
Let me here by your grace find my last earthly bed.

For weary my feet have all night paced the street;
And though hard is the brunt of the storm to be
          borne,
No kind glance can I meet, I can find no retreat,
To soothe the sad soul of poor ZAMPI forlorn.

Behold! how these white men in dwellings of pride,
On their soft, downy beds, sleep secure from the rain;
While I, the poor stranger, outside must abide,
In hunger and pain ; seeking death but in vain.

Some feast in their halls, and some revel and sing;
Some dance to the music of timbrel and drum;

Whilst to me, wretched thing, borne on memory's
    wing,
Their joy brings a sting while I think of my home.

In those sweet days of yore, when on Africa's shore,
I danced on the green with the young and the gay;
Oh! then I was blest — I shall be so no more!
Oh, then I was free and as happy as they!

No wretched and poor have been spurned from my
    door;
Nor left to lament in the storm and the cold.
They have slept on the very best mat on my floor;
For their feast I have told the best lamb of my fold.

"May the curse of the blighted —!" "Oh, hold!"
    I exclaimed;
"Son of Africa, curse not the land of the free,

We may well feel ashamed that, though Freedom's
    proclaimed
For all others, here pity alone is for thee."

I stretched out my hand — the poor African smiled
'Midst his tears, as he kissed it with grateful delight;
"From the storm raging wild, injured Africa's child,
I will find thee a shelter, and supper to-night!"

'Midst the torrents of rain and the tempest's wild
    roar,
We arrived at a door dear to man and to Heaven;
Where a refuge is sought — not in vain — by the
    poor;
And where to the FUGITIVE welcome is given!

It is thine, OWEN LOVEJOY! and thine are the
    deeds.
Thee alone of the throng I invoke to my song,
Which, wed to thy name, through all time that
    succeeds,
On the bright wings of fame shall be wafted along.

Yes, wafted on high, honored Lincoln, with thine,
The purest of stars in that galaxy bright,
Which, with love superhuman and justice divine,
Shall restore a lost race to humanity's light.

Behold! this poor African blessed by your care,
Falls prone in the dust to the Being unknown ;
And for you, in the fervor of true grateful prayer,
Invokes all the blessings that flow from his throne.

He exclaims: "Thou Great Spirit that rulest on
 high ;
Dread form that dost ride on the whirlwind and
 storm ;
When thou shakest the earth, and the sea, and the
 sky,
In thy mercy, spare those who thy mercy perform!"

THANKSGIVING DAY.

1859.

" My barns are full!" the rich man cries;
Whilst with his wealth he feasts his eyes,
" My stores o'erflow with wine and oil;
Henceforth my life is won from toil.
My soul, enjoy these blessings given,
This day we owe our thanks to Heaven."

Oh, sordid soul! canst thou not see,
Heaven has no answering smile for thee?
Think, think, perhaps this very night,
To distant realms thou take thy flight.
And then for thee life's sweets are flown;
Thyself left naked and alone!

What sounds shall then assail thine ear?
Sounds fit for fiends alone to hear;

Groans of the wretched, suffering poor,
Spurned by base menials from thy door;
Or cries of orphans whom thine hand
Despoiled, perhaps, of home and land;
Or sighs of widows in despair,
Bewailing, to the chill, damp air,
Those blessings which thine avarice
Diverted to thy private use.

Or if thou hast been high and great,
Thou bearest the thunders of the State
Lamenting, with a face confused,
That confidence thou hast abused;
And cursing her ungrateful son
Who wounds the breast he feeds upon.

Or, haply, thou hast money lent,
Sucking men's blood by cent. per cent.;
Regardless of a brother's pain,
Provided thou mayest reap the gain.
Oh, think what tortures shall assail
The usurer's soul; then, monster, quail!

Thy thanks are due to Heaven, dost say?
Why pay them, then, the other way?

Oh, Father, let my grateful heart
To thee its earnest wish impart;
For every blessing held in store
Let me be thankful evermore;
For health, for peace, for liberty,
But chief for honest poverty;
A conscience free from guilty stain
Of ill-got riches, false as vain.
And may I ever count it loss
To squander precious time for dross;
Or, baser still, in sordid play,
With men who shun the light of day;
Who quaff the maddening draught until
Their souls have lost all sense and will;
And their proud spirits, once so free,
Are chained in hopeless slavery!
Father, preserve both me and mine
From such a curse, by power divine!

But, rather, let my life be spent
Amassing wealth that brings content;
Pure wisdom from the ancient sages
Who lived in distant lands and ages;
Whose lore, than honey far more sweet,
Food for th' immortal soul is meet;
Philosophers and bards of old,
Whose precepts shine like purest gold.
Or let me woo the modest muse,
Whose charms the grovelling mass abuse;
Or trace the laws by which the spheres
Pour harmony on mortal ears.
Or, I those arts would learn to prize
Which charm, adorn and humanize.
But, chiefly, let my footsteps trace
Those scenes where sorrow veils her face;
And smooth the ruffled brow of care;
Misfortune's wrecks help to repair;
And learn, how blest it is to give,
Yea, far more blest than to receive!

AN AMERICAN SUNSET

1860.

> "Parting day
> Dies like the dolphin."— BYRON.

Oft have I sat hardby the sounding sea,
In those green isles which good Victoria rules,
And gazed with admiration on the sun
Bathing his golden tresses in the brine,
And flooding the sea and sky with rosy light.
Those scenes were beautiful, and filled my soul
Then fresh and hopeful from the hand of God,
With joys supreme, delights unspeakable!
But never have I seen, nor yet conceived,
In all my wild imaginings of beauty,
A scene more lovely, gorgeous or sublime
Than that which met my wondering gaze last night,
Here in this Western world, fair Illinois,
The youthful prairie State; ruled by no queen

Nor potentate; but by her noble sons
And queenly daughters; she herself a queen!

Oh glorious land!   Where else occurs a scene
Of such surpassing loveliness?   The sun
Had sunk behind the sombre Western woods,
All save a golden crescent of his orb;
The clouds around him piled in various shapes
Of towers and battlements, were lighted up
With gemlike rays, all blended and combined
With such consummate skill, no artist's hand
Would dare to emulate.   And then th' expanse
Of bright, ethereal sky that stretched between,
With every color tinged, displayed rich vales
As if of Ceres ripening in the sun;
Rich, golden tints with green and orange blent,
Which melted into seas of azure hue,
Studded with islands of celestial light;
Recalling to the soul those blissful days,
Or past or future, (for they are the same,)
When through Elysian fields it roamed at large,

And where forever it will freely roam ;
When passed the bridge connecting the two worlds;
The bridge of human life ; the golden link
That binds the past and future evermore.

See in the East, the mass of purple clouds
Reflects the glories of the setting sun ;
And on their brow, behold the bow of God
Is set in all its glory !   What a scene!
Oh life, oh light, oh heaven and earth and sky !
Why should we pine at fate, or pain or grief?
Why shrink at poverty and the cold glance
Of man, our happier brother here below ?
Or court his smile, or dread his wrathful frown ?
Since through fair Nature's charms we can commune
With the great Architect; and claim a share
In the inheritance of a Father's love ;
Rest in full confidence upon his arm ;
Bask in the sunshine of his countenance;
And thence imbibe a balm for every woe

NEW YEAR'S GREETING FOR 1861.

THE NORTH AND SOUTH MEET.

SOUTH.

Good morning, friend North, and a happy new year!
What news and what hopes do you bring?
Instead of rejoicing, we've reason, I fear,
To lament the approach of the spring;
No longer united our people now stand,
With brotherly love as before;
But in hostile array from far Maine's rocky strand
To famed California's gold shore.
Let us reason together, in hopes to avert
Those feelings that only can lead to our hurt.

NORTH.

'T is true, brother South, we no longer can boast
Of a Union, the hope of the world,

Wherever by mountain, or river or coast,
Our Stars and our Stripes were unfurled,
From the stormy Cape Horn to the shores of Japan,
From the gulf to the isles of the sea,
Man bowed to the triumph and glory of man,
And exclaimed "'T is the flag of the free!"
But now it is rent — though by no foreign foe;
The sons of fair Freedom have dealt her the blow!

SOUTH.

Yes! Lincoln, the rail-splitter, he did the deed;
(That name was not given in vain,)
For the Union he split, and our country must bleed,
And we bear the brunt and the stain.
And I must say, friend North, that you, too, lent
    your aid
And encouraged that venomous plan
By which old John Brown made that terrible raid,
To murder us all to a man,
By means of our slaves, whom he meant to let loose;
Now, North, is this right?   Have you any excuse?

NORTH.

Just hear me, friend South, although recrimination
I hate, for it cannot do good ;
Yet still, in the spirit of conciliation,
I would avert battle and blood ;
You blame "honest Abe," when, in truth, all the
  blame
Will be found to rest at your own door ;
Not content with digesting, in silence, your shame,
You must vaunt it the Nations before ;
And sully my fame dragged along with your own,
When you know both your crime and your shame I
  disown !

SOUTH.

What ! this to my face ? What ! a shame and a
  crime !
Dare you thus name our famed institution,
So hallowed by Scripture, prescription and time ?
Is this, then, the final solution ?

10

Is this, then, the only concession you make
To avert all the horrors of strife?
If so, from this garment defiance I shake;
And my challenge is, "War to the knife!"
Let slip all your bloodhounds; you 'll find me
     prepared;
My arm is equipped and my bosom is bared.

NORTH.

Well, South, be it so; you may strike, but first hear;
If love, then the Union, is flown;
Mere parchment is nothing, love only is dear,
And duty remains to be done:
Wherever that leads, I, for one, will pursue,
Regardless of what may befall;
To God and my country my service is due;
I will follow wherever they call.
But still I respect our relations in life,
If we cannot unite, let us part without strife.

We are brothers and kinsmen; and why should we
    steep
Our hands in each other's heart's blood?
Or why leave our widows and orphans to weep;
And our homes with destruction o'erflood?
Are the evils of life too infrequent and few,
That our hands must still add to their sum?
Are the last debts of nature so long overdue,
That our acts must invite them to come?
Oh pause, brother, pause in your frenzied career;
The world gazes on us in silence and fear!

SOUTH.

Why insult to injury add, brother North,
Why thus sugar-coat the deep wrong?
And why try to sully our honor and worth,
Because you presume you are strong?
From their masters you spirit our servants away,
Or if they escape from our land,
Despite of your compact, you throw in delay
To restore them; or justice withstand.

Do you think a brave, chivalrous people can yield

To such wrongs and such insults, and not take the
    field ?

NORTH.

We men of the North have long since washed our
    hands

Of the stain and the crime and the curse

That slavery brings.   Shall we heed your commands,

Though our friends, to do this and still worse ?

To pander to passions we hate and despise,

By becoming jackalls to catch slaves

For wolves and for tigers in human disguise ?

Think you, we are such servile knaves ?

If this be the cause that inflames you to fight,

Come on, and let God now decide for the right !

What, silent and pale !   Brother South, can it be

That your courage already is flown ?

A Pryor engagement, no doubt, you now see,

And the field of the Potter disown;
Well, well! you are prudent. The North may be
       duped,
As he has been, but will not "be dared!"
His bowie knife many a wame has out-scooped
And many a bosom, though "bared,"
So, fire-eating South, let me bid you good-bye:
Your courage is great, but we 'll make your wool fly!

ODE FOR THE NEW YEAR.

1862.

.

I tuned my harp to sing the passing year,
　And greet the coming one with joyous strain;
But ah ! its tones fell dead upon mine ear ;
　My efforts to awake them were in vain.

They slept in silence many a night and day,
　Until the waning year drew nigh its close;
Then, as its last sad moments rolled away,
　Strange, weird music from my lyre arose.

Two forms of heavenly mold — both fair and young,
　(One wreathed in smiles, and one in tears, I noted,)
Alternate woke the lay : — The words they sung
　I seized, as on the midnight air they floated.

SPIRIT OF THE OLD YEAR.

Fresh from the courts of Heaven, my sister fair,
  In youthful beauty and consummate grace,
To thee I yield this post of anxious care ;
  Assume the task and nobly fill the place.

SPIRIT OF THE NEW YEAR.

Why hangs that cloud upon my sister's brow,
  Where all was sweet and tranquil when we parted ?
How changed in form, in look, in gesture now !
  Tears in thine eyes, thou seem'st nigh broken-
        hearted.

SPIRIT OF THE OLD YEAR.

Alas ! dear sister, why must I relate
  The scenes of horror I have witnessed here ?
Or why did Heaven impose on me the fate
  To guide, in times so dread, this mundane sphere ?

My sisters fair who ruled the bygone years,
　　How man progressed on earth, would oft unfold;
And we, the spirits born to guard the spheres,
　　Exulted in the tidings which they told.

They said that light and darkness there contended
　　For mastery, and that the light prevailed;
That cruelty on earth was almost ended,
　　And despots in their fiendish schemes had failed;

That truth and justice were diffused abroad;
　　But chiefly in the Land of Liberty,
Where charity, the noblest child of God,
　　Would triumph soon and set the captive free.

But lately I have marked a deep'ning shade
　　Of gloom and sorrow on the brow of all;
Their hopes grew dim, their joys began to fade,
　　And horrors seemed their inmost souls to pall.

11

With dark forebodings I assumed my task,
    A year agone; my fears were too well founded;
Rebellion then had thrown aside the mask
    And stood revealed with all his fiends surrounded.

A horrid monster, dismal, dark, deformed;
    Drunk 'with much prosperity and crime:
With frenzied eye and iron tongue he stormed;
    His mouth all fire and foam, his beard all slime.

He grasped a dagger in his felon hand,
    And while his loving mother took her rest,
And her false guardian slumbered in the land,
    He sought to plunge it in her tender breast.

And when the Almighty Ruler turned aside
    The dastard blow; the monster aimed his dart
Against her sons, and dragged her flag of pride
    Soiled in the dust, thus wounding many a heart.

Then Lincoln, raised by Heaven to save the State,
    Good, honest Abe — the second Washington —
Stood up undaunted, bold, sublimely great,
    And, to avenge the mother, called each noble son.

They came obedient to the patriot's call,
    A mighty host disdaining fear or dread,
To cheer the loyal, rebels to appall ;
    The solid earth groaned 'neath their ponderous
        tread.

Their mustering might be likened to the hum
    Of myriad pigeons in the autumnal sky,
Heard in the distance ; till, at length, they come,
    With thundering wings, and rush impetuous by.

Then, with the cataract's tremendous roar,
    And with the raging. tempest's awful force,
Which hurls the howling billows on the shore,
    Our hosts sweep on in their resistless course.

On, on they sweep by myriads, each brave band
   Led by a dauntless chief; as Ellsworth brave;
As Lyon bold; as Baker brilliant, grand;
   (These, like Bielaski, found a hero's grave.)

And to rebellion cowardly and base,
   Safe only in his strongholds, they present
A wall of fire impervious in each place;
   To curb his madness seems their sole intent.

But Britain, jealous of the Nation's fame,
   And envious of her overshadowing glory,
Seeks every pretext to asperse her name,
   And 'rase her record from the world's great story.

How vain the effort! For that Babylon,
   That second Carthage steeped in perfidy,
Is doomed to fall before this youthful Rome;
   And as her crimes, so great her fall shall be.

But thou, sweet sister, say, what tidings good
  Dost thou to man from Heaven's bright portals
    bring?
Thy smile celestial and benignant mood
  Bespeak thee Herald of the Eternal King.

SPIRIT OF THE NEW YEAR.

To know the future rests with God above;
  Nor if I knew it dared I it impart,
Nor would it profit man.   That heaven is love
  Is truest science to the faithful heart.

Let Nature teach him.   As this ambient air,
  Impregned with vapors, must be purified;
So man estranged from God by sin and care,
  By tribulations must be sorely tried.

The storms of ocean keep its waters sweet;
  The earthquake saves the earth from latent fire;
The hostile clouds in fearful conflict meet,
  But yet their thunders in repose expire.

The epidemic which assails the young,
　　The burning fever preying on man's life,
Are sent the constitution to make strong,
　　And to prepare it for a nobler strife.

And so of nations.　God has called this forth
　　To serve some purpose, some most glorious end —
Of liberty to teach mankind the worth —
　　And human freedom everywhere extend.

And since corruption gathers in its veins,
　　Chokes its young heart, impedes its free-drawn
　　　　breath,
He sends his messengers to cleanse the stains,
　　And save the loved one from the threatened death.

When the corruptionists are swept away,
　　Whatever name or form they may assume;
When selfish politicians cease to sway,
　　And virtue's sun shines through the dark simoom;

When man shall act religion's great command,
  Love to his God and justice to his brother;
As each before Jehovah's throne would stand,
  So each be friend and neighbor to the other.

Then may the people hope for peace and rest,
  Nor longer suffer from the avenging rod;
Then shall the nation be supremely blest,
  And bask in sunshine, the sweet smile of God.

'T was thus they sung until their heavenly voices
  Were blended with the tones of earth's sweet bells,
Which raised to listening seraphs grateful noises,
  Whose anthem through the great cathedral swells.

Their words sank deep into my heart's recesses;
  Oh, may they yours with heavenly grace impress,
To love your brother, soothe his deep distresses;
  Serve God and country more, love SELF the less.

NEW YEAR'S ADDRESS.

1862.

With a Happy New Year, friends, once more I
    would greet you,
And say, I am always delighted to meet you;
To hold pleasant converse and gossip together —
Talk of politics, markets, the war and the weather;
And learn from their signs our frail life-boat to steer;
From experience draw wisdom and virtue each year;
Till prepared for the future, nor fearing the past,
An endless NEW YEAR shall burst on us at last,
Beyond all the changes and chances of time;
Where cold nor fierce heat mars the heavenly clime;
Where Spring reigns eternal and bright roses blow,
And the rivers of Eden with nectar o'erflow;
Where angels sweet music still pour on the air,
And all things renewed are celestial and fair!

Like the chorus of Greece, sounding solemn, sublime,
Teaching wisdom and wit with a chant or a chime,
The Carrier's Address makes you wise as you smile,
For it sparkles with wit and with humor the while;
Condensing past scenes to a span, to rehearse
Their essence in brief and embalm them in verse;
Till a favorite grown, nay, a fixed institution,
It purports to give you a happy solution
Of problems by statesmen and jurists propounded;
The ' whys ' and the ' wherefores' on which they are
   grounded;
The rocks on which candidates' barges are stranded;
How panics have left many folks empty-handed;
And why, though our garners with plenty are fraught,
The cup from our lips is dashed quicker than
   thought;
And why our brave troops, when well clothed and
   well fed,
Have failed of success, through defects of the Head:
The Carrier will tell you all this for a QUARTER,
Which is cheap, very cheap, for so great an
   exhorter;

Although on the quarter he lays little stress,

Some folks that are poor may be suited for less;

Nor would he much grumble, (rich friends, do not
laugh,)

If, instead of a quarter, you hand him a HALF!

Well, now for the message of which I have spoken,

In which you will find of his wisdom this token:

That, in order to lighten the gen'ral distress,

He presents to your view this, his annual address,

Replete with those maxims by which, duly followed,

Your cares and your sorrows will surely be swallowed

In perfect oblivion of war and disaster,

A plaster for broken hopes, yet no shinplaster!

"Come, quick with your nostrum!" you cry, in
suspense,

(Of which you are worthy in more than one sense,)

"Quick, quick, I'm impatient! What aid do you
    proffer?
Here's the money all ready — I close with your
    offer!"

Have patience, good sir, you will hear it at last;
The folks of our day are a 'leetle' too fast,
For dreading lest, haply, they should be too late,
They wait not the evil — but anticipate;
You may flout my reproof with a shrug or a leer,
But hark, I will whisper some truths in your ear!

Look around you, my friends, and what do you
    behold?
A land that flowed lately with silver and gold;
The earth groaned with plenty, the air breathed of
    health;
Our commerce proclaimed both our power and our
    wealth,
Expanded our empire from ocean to ocean,

To which all true hearts then proclaimed their
    devotion;
Our arts and our sciences flourished apace,
And the Nations we led in improvement's swift race;
The flood-gates of knowledge were open to all,
And the millions responded to Liberty's call;
Our presses diffused the good seed through the land;
Our patriots for freedom of speech made a stand;
Peace reigned through our borders, and war was
    unknown —
Save from far-distant rumor or fable alone.
These blessings and more were our lot here below,
You ask me, "Where are they?"   Pray, how should
    I know?
I am not a Solomon — a carrier am I,
Yet a query or two I 'll put in reply:

Shall we, the sole arbiters of our own fate,
Yield up to this sectional demon of hate,
And blot the best hopes of our race here on earth
By crushing the germs of all virtue and worth?
Shall the "model Republic" a by-word become,

While the Nations amazed are with horror struck
    dumb?
While Italy rallies her sons in the cause,
Shall we, in our Freedom's grand march, make a
    pause —
Unravel the web which our fathers have wrought,
Or look on while the fabric to ruin is brought?

No, never, by Heaven! while one arm shall remain
To combat disunion, its guilt and its stain!
No, never shall we sell our birth-right for gold,
Handed down by those heroes — our fathers of old!
The bare thought would arouse them from sleep in
    their graves
To curse us as cowards — disown us as slaves!
Let the traitors and fanatics fight for the prize
(Gold to such is a God — the sole light of their eyes)
Which the tempter holds out to debase and degrade,
They will snap at the bait and be caught — 't is their
    trade!
But the patriot's soul will forever be true

To that land where the first breath of freedom he
    drew,
Though the storm drive its wreck through the waves
    at its will,
He will love it the more and will cling to it still.
Then rally for Freedom — her hour draweth nigh;
For her we shall live, or with her we shall die!

We were told by base traitors, that this Constitution
Could no barrier oppose to a mad revolution;
That treason, rebellion and crime must go free,
And, unwhipt, blight the land with their wild
    anarchy.
Would Jackson thus talk? 'By th' Eternal,' not so!
Like lightning, his bolt would have laid treason low;
Ere the hydra had raised his fell head from the
    ground,
The monster its death-blow from him would have
    found.

Society can its own members restrain,
If fury or madness should seize on their brain;

And so can the States this rebellion control,
Since mad it would seek to dismember the whole;
But for this the great mass of good men must unite,
Since no ' section' nor 'faction' can cope with this
    fight;
And who denies this is a coward and slave,
Or, what is still worse, a base traitor and knave!

We all can remember the grief and surprise
Of our good UNCLE SAM — the big tears in his eyes,
When he saw his fine home by a bolt torn asunder;
How he called on Old Buck — then intent upon
    plunder!
Next Sam, in despair, called on Cass, but alas,
Faint echo perversely replied, "Where is Cass?"
Next, Uncle dived into his fob for his eagles,
And found they were plundered by placemen and
    beagles,
And with horror he saw, his hand still in his fob,
That they'd rifled his crib, nor e'en left him a Cobb!

But now the poor man has got nothing to say,

Though robbed by new Floyds and new Cobbs
  every day:

They abound high and low, and in every station —

In the army, the navy—throughout the whole nation;

Our soldiers they've cheated in stomach and body;

They've shod them with clouts, and they've clad
  them with shoddy!

So that Uncle, exhausted in funds by each job,

Will soon, it is feared, be left nothing to rob;

Even now his old garments are worn so threadbare

It is plain he will soon be left "nothing to wear;"

But he bears it right bravely — now wincing, now
  grinning,

His pains still decrease by the practice of skinning;

Till 'reft of all treasure, of sense e'en bereft,

Neither coat, breeks nor crib, Cobb or fob will be
  left!

And now, as historian, the Carrier will talk

Of affairs that took place here, at home on his walk;

What changes, improvements and scenes have
    occurred,
Since, one year ago, his report you have heard :
Our State was advancing in morals and wealth,
And our city was blessed with abundance and health ;
Till rebellion, the Upas-tree blighting our land,
(Whose shadow is death where its branches expand,)
Spread a gloom o'er our prospects, our hopes ren-
    dered vain,
And caused us to mourn for our patriots slain !
Oh, cursed be the wretch, north or south, east or
    west,
Who kindled or fann'd this fell flame in each breast !

As to scenes — the ELECTION produced a sensation,
And ' blue-lights' enough to enlighten the nation,
And GAS quite abundant was freely discharged,
To puff up our rivals and show them enlarged
Beyond all the bounds that Dame Nature intended ;
Such weapons and more were quite freely expended
In canvassing votes, both by bribes and corruption,

By whisky, by lies, and by secret seduction,

Till, Icarus-like, self-inflated and rash,

They burst up in mid air and came down with a
    crash!

But abuse of our candidates served but to raise

Honest friends to our cause — such abuse was their
    praise;

For while they to high honors in triumph were sent,

Their steps toward " Salt River " the Copperheads
    bent,

Their loss and discomfiture sadly to mourn;

But see, they come back! and we hail their return.

Reconciled to their fate, and good friends to the
    laws,

It is hoped they 'll now join in fair Liberty's cause;

And, forgetting the past, will make haste to unite

With the friends of the UNION, in faith and in right.

Well, now for a sermon: Last year brought about,

Like its fellows, strange scenes and some changes,
    no doubt,

Of joy and of sorrow, of pleasure and pain;
But one thing is clear, it will ne'er come again;
It is gone with the years that have passed since the
    flood,
But its record, alas, has been one traced in blood;
Yet the year that is on us our own we can make,
If time by the forelock we wisely shall take;
Improve every moment our minds to expand,
And diffuse noble principles over the land;
Enlighten men's darkness, relieve their distress,
And thus, blessing others, ourselves we shall bless;
And such is the aim of our present address!
Thus having accomplished our end and our aim,
Your smiles of approval and QUARTERS we claim;
Who give to the carrier lend the Lord who is just;
If you like the security, " down with the dust!"

" 'The dust!' pray, for what? Do you mean this
    to be a
Nostrum, a plaster, a sure panacea
For war, for disunion, secession and sorrow,

Which, threat'ning to-day, makes us sad for to-
morrow?

You promised to give us some balm at the close,

To soothe all our sorrows and heal all our woes;

Then, pray, why dismiss us with husks such as
those?"

What! ever to learn? Can you not comprehend?

Though so fast, you are slow — well, take this from
a friend,

My balm is this text, which I hope you'll improve:

QUITE ENOUGH FOR THE DAY IS THE EVIL THEREOF!

CARRIER'S ADDRESS.

Good friends, I am no politician,
  So I trust that you will me excuse
From wearing my brain by attrition,
  Since for you I am wearing my shoes.

I had hoped to get some one to write me
  A piece which your favors might win;
But the bards, one and all, seemed to slight me,
  Though I tried to inspire them — with TIN.

But my wife said to me, "Now, my honey,
  You have wit — why not put it to use?
If you can't turn your goose-quill to money,
  Why, then, you must be a great goose!

Look around — there is Tom, Dick and Harry,
   Once ditchers, and choppers, and sawyers;
See how high now their sheeps' heads they carry,
   As editors, doctors and lawyers!"

Thus bantered and urged on by Nancy,
   I plunge in! Do you wish me to scan
The acts of Floyd, Davis, Cobb, Yancey,
   And relate how the strife first began?

Well, you know that Miss Kansas, our cousin,
   Once had suitors from North and from South,
From East and from West, by the dozen;
   But for none would she open her mouth.

Then her guardian, Old Buck, waxed quite rusty,
   And said he, " You must wed, I declare —
Do n't turn up your nose nor get crusty;
   Do n't you see I am wanting an heir?

There 's a gallant of NIGHTLY extraction,
    Lays himself and his — slaves at your feet;
He loves you — he swears to distraction!
    What better could suit you, my sweet?"

But Kansas was callous or cunning,
    And she turned up her nose as before;
And said she, " Uncle Buck, you 're but funning,
    And, besides, I another adore!"

" Pooh, nonsense! Young girls read romances,
    And think themselves able to judge,
When, in truth, their best thoughts are wild fancies;
    I will teach you good sense! This is fudge!"

Now it chanced that her old tutor, "DUGGY,"
    Came up in the midst of this scene,
And he rode in his own one-horse buggy,*
    And he drove in his buggy between.

*The Kansas-Nebraska Bill.

And said he, " Brother Buck, this is cruel;
    Shall the girl have no will of her own?
Do n't you know she 's my pet and my jewel?
    I shall never my pupil disown!

I have promised her, times without number,
    She should never be forced in her choice;
And now I 'm resolved not to slumber,
    Till her friends all respond to my voice."

Thus her voice became free, unrestricted,
    And the North, her TRUE lover, she chose.
And hence we 've been sorely afflicted;
    From this source all our troubles arose.

For the NIGHT-errant, fire-eating suitor,
    Who before by her beauty was smitten,
Swore vengeance 'gainst her and her tutor,
    The moment she gave him the mitten.

And he issued a roving commission
   To Floyd, Yancey, Davis and Cobb,
To proceed quick, without intermission,
   His rival to rifle and rob.

So they stole many small arms and cannon,
   And him of some strong-holds bereft;
And no doubt they 'd have robbed Jim Buchanan
   Of his soul — if he 'd had any left!

And at Sumter, Bull Run and Ball's Bluff,
   He dealt us hard knocks, I admit;
But we soon made him hollow, "Enough!"
   At Donelson, Shiloh, to wit.

But while those with brave Grant, Pope and Siegel
   Were pounding the rebels, out West;
At Richmond our MUD-TURTLE eagle
   Was intrenching himself in his nest.

And said he, " I had rather encounter
　　The foe with my spades than my guns."
Now such EAGLES we nail to the counter,
　　As COUNTERFEIT NAPOLEONS.

'T is a left-handed kind of ambition,
　　When a Gen'ral cooped up in his hole,
Like a bear, will not change his position
　　Until poked in the ribs with a POLL.

And that poll will tempt him to his ruin,
　　To climb towards the President's chair;
Till, swept from his feet, it leave Bruin
　　To wallow once more in his lair!

This mighty Napoleon of Hardshells
　　Could ne'er be induced to advance
While there lacked but one spade to his mud-sills,
　　Or their pants lacked one button by chance.

Let 'em slide — since more worthy succeed them,
  Brave Burnside, McClernand and Banks ;
And others will rise as we need them,
  To fill and adorn Freedom's ranks.

For the God of our Fathers ordains it,
  That Freedom reign through our whole realm ;
And by virtue and valor maintains it,
  While LINCOLN presides at the helm.

Undaunted, he clings to his station,
  Through the storm guides the good Ship of State;
His watch-words, " HOPE, EMANCIPATION !"
  Triumphant o'er foemen and fate!

Yes, Lincoln, steer on in thy glory,
  Be Freedom thy pole-star on high;
And thy name, both in song and in story,
  Shall blaze while yon sun fires the sky!

Now, of home and the changeable breezes,
    You wish me to tell you some saws:
When the wind blows right cold, then it freezes;
    When the sun shines out warm — then it thaws.

And when the fierce war-fever rages,
    The Democrats all catch the chills ;
But when an election engages
    Their thoughts, they forget all their ills,

And crawl from their dusky recesses,
    Driven forth by the demagogue's lash.
Some through whisky commit great excesses;
    Some vote for SECESH — some for CASH.

And then they call this " a reaction,"
    " A great revolution," forsooth!
When 't is only the fang of the faction,
    Which can't bite, though it still shows its tooth.

I might add — but I feel quite deficient,
   (Practice only makes perfect they say,)
Yet I think I have told you sufficient
   Your "quarters" to conjure away.

"Odds-zooks, man! the times are too dreadful,
   And quarters are not to be had;
For the war-tax has swallowed the needful,
   And the Carrier's chances are bad."

Hold, sir! Lend an ear to my story;
   For the Carrier you then will decide;
If the fine arts form part of your glory —
   Home production a part of your pride.

There was once an old tribe of PRECISIANS;
   (They were Danites, I dare to suppose,)
Who long suffered for lack of provisions,
   Till a Genius amongst them arose.

This worthy first taught them back-gammon,
    (It was gammon, or cheat, some say chess,)
Which made them oblivious of famine,
    And greatly assuaged their distress.

To his memory, 't is said, they erected,
    ('T is now all in ruins,) — a mound ;
Now more worthy than his, if dissected,
    My merits will surely be found.

If from war-tax I draw your attention,
    Shut out debts and duns from your view —
Mine is likewise a happy invention,
    And worth a remembrancer too.

Truly, wit is a mighty exhorter,
    For I see you have laughed yourselves fat;
Now as freely you deal out your quarter,
    May your duns deal you QUARTER for that.

THE POWER OF MUSIC.

INSCRIBED TO

PATTI AND GOTTSCHALK,

HEARD IN CONCERT AT SPRINGFIELD, JANUARY 8, 1863.

Of Orpheus and Arion ye have heard;
One by his music charming trees and rocks
To dance, enraptured, to his magic art;
Compelling Pluto, in the shades below,
Th' inexorable law of fate to o'errule,
And yield him up Euridice, his wife:
The other, by the touches of his lyre,
Joined to the thrilling accents of his song,
The dolphins from the ocean's depths alluring
To sport delighted 'round the unfriendly bark
Whose murderous crew, impelled by thirst of gold,
Like swine, regardless of the precious freight
They bore in company, conspired to rob
The minstrel of his treasure and his life;

Granting this simple boon, sought by his prayer:
That he once more might tune his harp to sing
A parting song of peace, a funeral dirge,
To soothe his spirit on its march of death.

And how he sang, you 've heard —: how from the
　　depths
Of ocean and its coral caves there sprung
A wondrous audience.　As, at dead of night,
When the alarm-bell strikes the sleeping ear,
And calls the citizens to rouse themselves
And save their cherished homes from fire or sword;
They rush, they hasten to whatever spot
The danger threatens: — So the finny tribes,
Sleeping in shady caverns of the deep,
Roused by th' unwonted tones, spring forth and rush
Impetuous towards the spot whence flow the sounds,
And there remain enchanted, till the close.
A pause succeeds — when hark! a sullen splash,
At which the monsters of the deep take flight;
All, save the dolphins, as by instinct taught,

That the sweet music flows from source divine,
And that the minstrel needs their friendly aid.
So, as Arion with his sounding lyre
Is sinking in the wave, they, like true friends,
Subject their backs beneath and buoy him up;
And waft their precious burden to the shore!

Nor deem these fables vain; nor disbelieve,
Because they seem of miracles compact.
They have their uses and significance.
Besides, ART is a miracle more strange,
More inconceivable to clods of clay,
Than any in the saintly calendar!
Nature produces wonders, but requires
Much time and space her mysteries to unfold;
She works by gradual sequences, and groups
Her various works in many lands and climes.
But Art is, like to God, omnipotent
And omnipresent; and, like Him, creates,
From scattered and disjointed elements,
Whole worlds of beauty and magnificence

To charm the sense and teach th' immortal soul,
Thirsting for knowledge, great, undying truths.

'T is thus the Muse of history and song
Recalls the by-gone ages to our mind,
And marshals them before our wondering eyes.
'T is thus the painter and the sculptor cull,
From Nature's field of color and of form,
The concentrated essences of all
That is most lovely and most exquisite
In individuals or single groups,
In order to produce, in all its parts,
A new creation, blending every charm
Of nature's favorite mold, and lacking none.
Whoever shall in this great art excel,
He is a master, and on him the world
The God-like name of Genius will confer.

Gottschalk, to thee this name is justly due ;
Who, by thy wondrous mastery o'er sounds,

Unaided by articulate speech, hast formed
A new creation of thine own; a world
Of miracles; a paradise of sweets;
That more than realize the dreams of old,
The witchery of Orpheus in the woods,
Or of Arion 'midst the finny tribes;
And, aided by the siren, Patti's voice,
Not only canst thou move the trees and rocks;
Charm the mute fishes in their liquid homes;
But thou canst change the seasons in their course,
And mold the mood or landscape at thy will!

Entranced I listened as the change went on;
And felt through every nerve the influence
Of each successive change like one who dreams
Of Paradise and dreads lest he awake!

The winter's sullen gloom, the snow-clad earth,
The streams in icy fetters strongly bound,
The leafless forests moaning in the blast,
Are touched by magic of the master's hand

Or siren's voice, and lo! bright sunny skies
With trees of richest verdure, laughing brooks
Singing through meadows rich with the perfumes
Of new-mown hay, and roses greet my sense.
The landscape smiles around; the warblers pour
Their choicest melodies; the nightingale
As emulous of Patti's peerless strain,
Redoubles all her efforts to excel,
Till overcome, she dies from grief and shame;
While pitying zephyr moans amongst the leaves,
Now soft, now loud, as grief or rage prevail.
Anon, with mighty sweep the rising storm,
Rushing resistless through the shrieking woods,
Now nearer comes and nearer, till, at length,
It bursts in fearful thunder o'er our heads,
And seems to rend the solid earth in twain;
At length its voice in softest whispers dies,
And, mingling with the babbling fountain's song,
To sweet repose invites the weary soul.

Anon, the bells from some fair village chime
The vesper hour; at which the hum of prayer,

The organ, mingled with the evening hymn,
Are heard to float aloft to listening Heaven.
The cattle low responsive to their young;
The snowy flocks with their sweet tinkling bells
Browse happy on the plain.   Their bleating lambs,
Emblems of innocence, partake their bliss,
And frolic round them in excess of joy.

And hark that joyous strain!   'T is Rachelette
Who sings her rustic song with lightsome heart,
While her tall, knightly lover sighs in vain!
Oh, what a harmony of mingling sounds!
Through which the maiden's strain may still be heard
Distinct, as silver threads appear more bright
In contrast with the sombre velvet warp;
Or as pure streamlets through dark landscapes gleam;
Luxuriant landscapes in some happy isle!

And now we hear the Ojos' joyous songs,
Who bask in sunshine in the fair Antilles,

The blood of old Castile — whose melodies
Seemed blended of the mingled tones of flutes,
Of flageolets and piccolos, with strains
Of thrushes, finches, nightingales and all
The sweet-voiced minstrels of the world combined;
Yet each distinct, a wild and wondrous maze!

Another change!   Grim Darkness spreads her wings;
We hear them flapping on the murky air;
And the dull welkin echoes them with sighs.
We hear the warring of the elements;
The clouds are gathering and the pattering rain
Begins to fall in heavy, measured drops
And solemn foot-fall o'er us on the roof.
But soon it thickens : — down the torrent pours;
The swollen gutters murmur as they run;
And from the eaves the water bubbles fast —
Now rushes down in torrents :   Standing aghast,
I seek a place of shelter — but in vain!
The flood increases — now it is a sea!
And on its bosom what do I behold?

A lovely bark with sails all set and free
Quick bounding o'er it, like a thing of life!
And on its lofty deck what do I see?
A minstrel, and a maid as angel fair,
Who flood the air with music — all the tribes
Of ocean listen to the melting lay.
Then comes a pause — and then a crash is heard —
I start in terror!   Can this be a dream?
The dolphins bear upon their faithful backs
The minstrels through the wave of wild applause,
And land them on the solid rock of Fame!

THE POWER OF ELOQUENCE.

Inscribed to Gen. R. J. Oglesby,

On hearing his great Union Speech in Representatives Hall, in
Springfield, Ill., January 9, 1863.

Brave Oglesby, I thank the Lord my God,
That I have lived to realize this truth,
That patriotic and heroic hearts,
Wise heads, and tongues of burning eloquence,
Are still amongst us — still prepared to stem
The fearful flood of anarchy and crime
Which threatens to o'erwhelm us — and that we,
The people, still retain the instinctive love
For truth and justice which our honored sires
Bequeathed to us — the noblest legacy.

Assembled in our capital the chiefs,
Devoted to their country and their God,

Were seated in council, to deliberate
Upon our Nation's perils and our own;
Assailed by open enemies abroad,
And threatened by pretended friends at home.
The citizens stood densely crowded round,
And beauty graced the galleries.   A strain
Of patriotic music filled the hall;
And scarcely had its echoes died away,
When many hundred voices cried at once
The name of " Oglesby."   The hero rose
Slow and majestic, suffering still from wounds
Received by him at hard-fought Donelson,
Where he had poured his blood in Freedom's cause;
And where his life he would have sacrificed
To save his country from its threatened doom;
But God the will accepted for the deed,
And, by a miracle, preserved that life
For future efforts in her sacred cause!
In him his fellow citizens beheld
Their beau ideal of the hero-race —
A MAN of true nobility of soul;

And recognizing his great worth, with cheers
Loud and prolonged they greeted his address:

"My fellow citizens:" the hero cried,
"If we would be successful in this war,
We must renounce whatever might divert
Our purpose for a moment to crush out
This foul conspiracy, this causeless wrong
Against our country and humanity.
We must renounce all selfishness, and yield
All thoughts of aggrandizement for a while ;
And be true patriots, both in name and deed.
Why then those sullen mutterings which we hear
Of grovelling wretches fearing to be taxed
A portion of their substance, to sustain
The noblest structure which this world has seen;
The pride, the boast, the glory of the world ?
Do any grudge a part to save the whole ?
What were our wealth without a government
Strong to defend and willing to protect
Each citizen in his inherent right ;

His life, his substance and his liberty?
Are these worth nothing?   Will no sacrifice
Of present comfort or of future wealth
Be made these glorious blessings to secure
To us and our posterity forever?
Would any grudge a half to save the whole?
Yet, should this war for ten long years prevail,
Not e'en one tenth would ever be required;
And who amongst us would refuse a tenth
To render life and all it gives secure?

As citizens we have undoubted right
The acts of public servants to discuss;
But no man has a right, in times like these,
Against the lawful, constituted powers,
Whose aims are right, whose purposes are just,
A factious opposition to maintain,
Injurious to the welfare of the State,
Or such as should give comfort to its foes.
And if there be in Illinois to-night
Such characters as I here indicate,

Then brand them traitors to their country's cause,
And bitter enemies to God and man.
At least permit me to assert this much,
That knowing Abraham Lincoln as I do,
Were I to throw obstructions in his path
Whilst laboring for my good, I should betray
A captious spirit and a little mind,
Unworthy of a soldier and a man.
I speak but for myself; for no one else!
I recognize no narrow party ties;
I claim no sympathy with factious men.
My country claims my heart, my life, my all!
The great, grand Union party! that is mine,
And that alone, my country and my God!
Our noble President demands our praise,
And how can we refuse it, being just?
While living here amongst us well we knew
And recognized his worth. As "honest Abe"
We hailed him then; and is he prone to change?
No, no! he does not change! his heart is right;
Although, as being mortal, not a God,
His judgment may be liable to err;

Yet, if an Angel ever blessed our earth —
A stranger to corruption and to pride;
Grand in his pure nobility of soul;
Of innate dignity, unselfish heart,
And firm, unswerving purpose to do right:
In Abraham Lincoln such might well be found.
We all remember when that great, good man
('Tis now two years ago,) took leave of us,
The duties of his office to assume ;
How deep the sympathy, how warm the prayers
Of all who knew him were for his success ;
And how, surrounded by his country's foes,
Assailed, at every step, with calumny,
And threatened by the assassin's bloody knife —
His country torn with faction and dismembered —
He entered the Nation's Capitol and assumed
The reins of government, with port sublime,
A courage which the consciousness of right,
The purpose to redress his country's wrongs,
And rule with justice and humanity,
Alone could have imparted, through his God.
And thus confiding in his righteous cause,

And in the blessing of approving Heaven,
He ever since has followed in the course
He then marked out.   And who will dare to say
He ever, for a moment, turned aside
From that strict path of right; so far, at least,
As human judgment may decide?   For me,
I shall be slow to censure or condemn
A man of such nobility of soul;
E'en though through human frailty he may err;
"To err is human; to forgive, divine."
Be slow, my friends, to censure generous hearts;
Be slow our honored Lincoln to condemn!

The love of country is a privilege
Which all men may enjoy.   To fight for it,
The greatest boon bestowed on mortal man,
Is one which is vouchsafed but to the few.
'T is incommunicable — it is supreme,
Unspeakable, absorbing in itself
The greatest good that man can reach below;
An earnest and a foretaste of the bliss

The ransomed and redeemed enjoy in Heaven!
When glorious victory crowns the patriot's toil;
When, in the midst of carnage and of death,
The bloody struggle for the Nation's life,
The foe is crushed; and on their prostrate works,
His comrades cheering him with wild huzzas,
He plants triumphantly the Stars and Stripes,
There is a feeling grander, more sublime
Than any other which the heart can feel;
Which none can know save those whom Heaven
    vouchsafes
The dangers and the triumphs to partake!

How mean, how paltry, in such scenes as these,
Do politics and party strife appear!
Shall I refuse my comrade's proffered hand,
Baptised in rebel blood, and consecrate
To glory in the sacred cause of Right,
Because, forsooth, he differed from my creed
In politics or faith, in times gone by,
And differs now; but yet who by my side

Fights like a brother in a common cause,

Which knows no bigot or sectarian creed:

No party, save the brotherhood of men,

Shedding their blood for Union and the Right?

Shame, shame on those vile dastards, cowards, slaves,

Who skulk at home from danger, and who sow

The seeds of faction and of discord 'twixt

Those noble spirits, who have laughed at fear,

And, shoulder to shoulder, braved the cannon's

    mouth!

For what? That traitors might assail their rear

From covert batteries, within whose screen

They belch their treason; for a time secure,

As they imagine! or who will not make

The smallest sacrifice for Fatherland,

In this, its hour of danger and of woe;

But hinder others in their patriot work!

If such there be in Illinois, to-night,

Hear me, ye semiloyal! such men sink

Themselves in deep damnation; yea, so deep

That no redemption e'er can reach them there —

They sink to ruin and can rise no more!

My fellow citizens, be reassured;

Be not deceived, ye traitors, but beware:

If, for a moment, the great public heart

Of this proud people seems to sink or quail,

'T will soon revive and reassert itself,

And, through its own elastic force, resume

Its normal state and crush the foe to dust!

That mighty heart is right, and ever beats

In unison with justice, freedom, truth;

Nor will it rest, until a glorious peace

Is conquered, and rebellion hides its head

In its own hell, whence it no more can rise

To scourge our country with its scorpion sting.

And citizens, forget not those who fight

Your battles in the field; encourage them

By word and deed, and cheer their faithful hearts,

To bear their hardships and privations, such

As few here reck of.   Help their families;

Let not the wives and children of the brave

Suffer at home, while sire and husband fight

For you and yours, and all that you hold dear;

And aid your noble Governor whose time,
Whose matchless energy, whose skill and care,
Have been unceasingly applied, to help
The soldier and the cause for which he fights !
Yea ! Richard Yates has nobly done his part !
To him the country and his native State
Are deeply bound in gratitude and love ;
And every soldier and his family,
Within the bounds of our illustrious State,
Has cause to call down blessings on his head.
And he who would malign him for this cause,
Acts from the impulse of a traitorous heart ;
And infamy shall be his just reward,
So long as man can judge of right and wrong.

You ask my views of that much talked of act,
By which so many millions of our race
Are to humanity and its rights restored ;
And what the Army thinks about the same.

What all our troops may think 't were hard to say,
But with those portions of them which I know,

The act is popular.   They think it right
That those whose aim it is to take their lives,
By means of guns or slaves, should be deprived
· Of either instrument, or both.   They feel
But slight compunction to deprive the foe
Of murderous weapons, whether steel or slaves,
Or anything that gives the rebels strength :
They do not think that rebels should enjoy
(Although they be slave-owners) sacred rights
In human bones and sinews, paramount
To those which soldiers have in self-defense ;
Who would their country and her rights protect
Against the aggression of those rebel hordes;
Nor would they weep to see the dagger snatched
From out th' assassin's hand.   A soldier, too,
I coincide with them.   The Southern States
Spurn all our overtures, while they employ
Their slaves to our destruction, like their guns.
Why, then, I cannot recognize their right
To kill me with their slaves, or with their swords,
But would of both disarm them !   What say you?

I 'm answered by your cheers! — the argument
Has hit the mark. 'Tis well, my friends! Good
   night."

How awful is the power of eloquence!
How mighty and tremendous is the right!
How irresistible the power of truth,
Issuing like two-edged sword from righteous lips!
How scathing are the bolts of argument,
In justice hurled against rebellious heads!
How terrible the wounds which they inflict!
More terrible than those which mighty Jove
Inflicted on the Titans who piled up
Pelion on Ossa, that their impious crew
Might scale the walls of Heaven! More terrible
Than those inflicted by th' arch-angel's sword
On Satan and his rebel host, cast down
From bliss of Paradise to deepest hell.

'T was thus the noble soldier-citizen,
Resistless in the forum as the field,

Hurled thunderbolts of truth and shells of flame
Against those vile and sordid men who seek
For power and station in their Country's fall;
Who glory in her worst calamity.
Nor ceased his batteries to play until
The dastard horde, the conscience-stricken crew,
Writhing with torture visible to all,
Shrank back affrighted into nothingness,
The scorn and laughing-stock of all mankind.

How grand, majestic, did the hero seem,
Expanding to the stature of a god,
As warmed, he rose with his tremendous theme!
All sense of suffering was laid aside;
All memory of marches, hardships, wounds;
And nothing save his Country and her woes
Remembered in that glorious hour sublime;
And as the wind sweeps o'er the watery plain,
Stirring its billows to their utmost depths,
His eloquence so stirred the hearts of men,
And molded to his will.   A surging wave

Of human beings, rolling to and fro,
In sympathy with every word he spoke,
Could scarce restrain their feelings till the close
Of each bold climax gave the pent-up force
A license to explode in wild applause;
And then the roof and distant welkin rang
With peal on peal; and angels stooped to bear
The grateful incense to the throne of God.

Well can we realize th' historic truths
Transmitted to our day through every age,
How Eloquence, the child of Liberty,
Has ever labored in her sacred cause.
How Pericles aroused his native land
To deeds immortal, by his burning words;
And how Demosthenes, devoid of arms,
Save those which truth and eloquence supplied,
Kept wily Philip and his hordes at bay,
And saved his country; how, at ancient Rome,
The listening forum echoed Tully's voice,
Denouncing tyranny with matchless power,

Or calming the wildest passions to repose;
These noble truths we now can make our own,
Since Oglesby has taught us here to-night
The boundless power of eloquence and truth.

Judge not the master's eloquence, my friends,
By this imperfect sketch, this skeleton
Of what he uttered .   Nor, could I impart
His every word, should ye e'en judge from them
The power he wielded; since, in eloquence,
Much on the speaker's manner must depend ;
His look, his gesture and the sacred flame
By which he is inspired.   'T was nobly said
By Æschines, when, by his scholars praised
For splendid reading of that brilliant speech,
By which himself was vanquished : " Ah, my
          friends,"
He said, " I thank you for your kind applause;
But had you heard Demosthenes himself,
Deliver that which I but feebly read,
How great your admiration would have been !
How rapturous your thunders of applause!"

HYMN FOR THANKSGIVING DAY.

1863.

How can we raise our thoughts to thee,
　Our Father and our God?
Or from thy wrath where can we flee,
　Or thy avenging rod?
Our cup of woe is flowing o'er,
Our Country bleeds at every pore.

O God, our Father, we confess
　Ours is the guilt and shame;
While thy kind hand was stretched to bless,
　We spurned thy sacred name:
Thy goodness and thy love forgot,
Or scorned, as if remembered not.

To thee, for all thy mercies shown,
    What tribute did we bring?
We hugged an idol of our own,
    Who ruled our hearts as king;
To him our thoughts, our all were given,
While thee we mock'd, and scoff'd at Heaven!

The widow and the fatherless
    We sorely have oppressed;
And those already in distress,
    We have still more distressed;
Our greedy hands have seized the prey,
Gold, gold must come, come whence it may.

And to attain it, we have brayed,
    In brazen mortars strong,
The limbs of men whom we had flayed,
    Nor deemed the deed was wrong;
We've melted in the furnace flame
Their hearts, nor thought it sin nor shame!

And if a wretch escaped the rack,
   We credit claimed from God,
That to his hell we drove him back,
   And to the avenging rod.
Our noblest aim, our chief desire,
Seemed, how to fan the despot's fire.

We 've said, 't was constitutional,
   A RIGHT, oh Lord, from thee;
Our DUTY, men thus to inthrall,
   A CRIME to set them free;
And with our offerings coined from blood,
Before thy altar we have stood,

And cried, with sanctimonious face,
   " Behold, oh Lord, we bring
These tithes, extorted, by thy grace,
   From human suffering.
Accept the tribute soaked in gore,
And bless us now as heretofore !"

Hark! God responds in thunder tones
   Of fierce and raging wars;
Our plains deformed with human bones;
   Our sons with wounds and scars;
Inflicting woes on every hand,
Fell Desolation stalks the land!

Oh God, forgive us! Low in dust
   Thy mercy we implore;
In thee, THEE only, is our trust,
   Thy smile to us restore;
Make us and our great country free,
And all the glory be to thee.

'T is done! We bless thee that, at length,
   The raging plague is stayed;
That thou hast risen in thy strength,
   In majesty arrayed,
And, through thy servant, hast proclaimed
An act that maketh not ashamed.

Oh Lord, for this accept our praise;

   For this we raise the song.

Grant Abraham Lincoln length of days,

   His arm make firm and strong;

And generations yet unborn

Shall bless thee each Thanksgiving morn!

EPITHALAMIUM,

.

On the Marriage of Maj. Gen. John A. McClernand to Miss Minerva
Dunlap, at Jacksonville, Ill., December 23, 1862.

INSCRIBED TO MRS. McCLERNAND.

Lo, Hymen, with his torch divine,
   With happy omen — sacred rite,
   True lovers deigneth to unite;
   Bright Venus and the Loves attend,
   The Graces too their presence lend,
And Hebe pours the wine.

'T is happy when the brave and fair
   Thus join with heart in hand,
   When sympathy draws close the band;
   When virtue, wisdom's mild control,
   Blends with true love in each true soul,
And finds its treasure there.

16

Then doubly happy be the hour
   When Mars and Venus meet;
   That union must be strong and sweet
   Where beauty, wisdom, grace and truth,
   In matchless form and blooming youth,
Unite with worth and power.

" The brave alone deserve the fair,"
   Was said in days of old;
   A truth our own age has retold
   In many an epos yet unsung,
   Which Fame's undying, ceaseless tongue
Will waft upon the air.

Yes! she will sing through all the world,
   In each succeeding age,
   And paint on the historic page
   The record of McClernand's deeds,
   'Gainst those by whom his country bleeds,
Who fierce defiance hurled.

Who first in Congress raised his voice
   Against the rebel band,
   And for his country took his stand,
   Regardless of the frenzied cries
   Of traitors, linked by party ties —
His country his first choice.

And having, in her sacred cause,
   Exhausted eloquence,
   As Chatham's manly, bold, intense,
   Such as might rival Tully's fame,
   Or old Demosthenes' pure flame,
No longer stood to pause,

But o'er the toga girt the sword,
   And boldly took the field,
   Determined not to shrink nor yield;
   And Belmont's fiery fray can tell —
   And Shiloh, Donelson, how well
He kept his plighted word.

And thou, Minerva, didst regard,
  With woman's faithful eyes,
  Thy hero struggling for the prize ;
  His country first to save, he strove,
  And thus secure thy noble love,
And lo, his rich reward !

Both prizes crown his laurelled brow!
  Both triumphs he hath won!
  The fight which hath been well begun
  Is certain of a glorious end ;
  Minerva, be his help and friend,
Henceforth, as then and now !

LILY BELLE.

An Angel came beneath our roof to dwell,
So fair was she, we named her LILY BELLE;
She won all hearts — we loved her, oh, how well!

Her form was clothed in every winning grace;
Pure love was mirrored in her radiant face,
Where all the budding virtues we could trace.

And oh, the luster of her matchless eyes,
Which flashed upon the soul a strange surprise —
Earth's violets blent with azure of the skies!

The rich luxuriance of her golden hair
Veiled, like a cloud, her brow and bosom fair,
Or streamed in wavelets to the breezy air.

Each day she grew in wisdom more and more;
Her tiny feet made music on our floor;
Her voice had thrilled our souls full oft before.

But ah! some sentinel at Heaven's gate,
Whose eye was keen, whose love was passing great,
Had seen our fair, and wooed her for his mate.

Our LILY drooped her head upon her breast;
She seemed to pine for some bright vision blest;
Then looked ADIEU, and sped to love and rest.

She's left us desolate. The strife is o'er;
Her spouse receives her on you heavenly shore,
Where we shall join her soon — to part no more!

THE IMPENDING BATTLE.

That thrilling sound!   It is the bugle's breath,
Which wakes our hosts to victory or death!
The drum beats loud "To arms!" the soldiers start,
And seize their weapons with a bounding heart;
Their dreams of home and loved ones distant far,
Yield to the stern realities of war.
Ah! which can tell if Sol's all-cheering ray
For him shall gild the scene another day?
Ah! which can tell if eve's soft shade shall steep
His sense in Nature's, or in Death's cold sleep!

And lo! their bayonets glance in morning's light,
And sweet Aurora shudders at the sight;
A gloomy horror palls each mortal sense,
And e'en the river murmurs in suspense,

As conscious that, ere night, his lucid flood
Shall roll deep dyed with his own children's blood ;
For two vast hosts, like hostile clouds, advance
To meet in civil strife.   Their helmets glance,
And wave their plumes, as grass waves in the breeze,
Ripe for the scythe ; or, like the forest trees
Ere winter sweeps them bare.   And now behold,
They stand erect, their arms like burnished gold,
Bright gleaming in the sun — a gallant sight,
Did patriotism their souls as one unite
In the great cause of Right and Liberty,
For then the world combined they might defy ;
But ah ! lament with me the fatal day,
When mad ambition led his dupes astray !

See, bearing messengers from rank to rank,
Fleet steeds are hurrying ; and the frequent clank
Of swords is heard, as aids fly swift along ;
Around dark tubes of death behold a throng
Of warriors cluster — there they ready stand,
Each cannonier a lighted torch in hand,

To fire the fatal train that instant hurls
Destruction in its track! Our host unfurls
The glorious Stars and Stripes; while theirs displays
That emblem which deceives while it betrays:
The stillness that precedes the storm is there,
Till hark! our chieftain's voice rings on the morning
  air:

"Soldiers and fellow citizens:" he cried,
" This day the fate of millions will decide!
This day you must make good your country's claim
To Freedom, or renounce the Freeman's name!
Behold the foe arrayed before your eyes;
There foul Rebellion stands without disguise;
There Treason midst a horde of despots stalks,
And shameless there the frequent Arnold walks,
And simulates of man the noble heart,
As if prepared to act the hero's part;
As if the perjured wretch, the dastard knave,
(Only in lies and deeds of darkness brave,)
Could awe the patriot's soul or strike him down,
When he can scarcely hide his scathing frown,

17

His fiery glance — then how shall he withstand
His lightning bolt or his red flaming brand?

Let this great truth be on your minds impressed,
The bravest man is he whose cause is best;
For he whose cause will not endure the sun,
May fight a while, but in the end must run,
Or yield his dastard life a worthless prize;
He cannot long sustain his dark disguise;
His gasconade will burst in thinnest air;
And all his native baseness be laid bare;
Himself a mere poltroon! Despair alone
Dictates the traitors' course, and drives them on
To swift destruction. Lo, within their lines,
The thief in stolen splendor blushless shines;
The robber and the assassin point the guns
Stolen from the mother, at her loyal sons!
There the marauder and the pirate stand
Prepared to waste and plunder this fair land;
Murder her sons, her daughters force to shame;
And bring disgrace on her unsullied name.

Was it for this our Western world was won
From ocean's wave? redeemed by Washington?
Her institutions by high Heaven inspired?
Her sons by patriot flame so nobly fired
To deeds of daring, glorious and sublime,
As any on the scroll of bygone time?
That British tyrants quailed before their frown;
And the whole earth still echoes their renown!
And shall you yield the prize your fathers won?
And shall each godlike sire disown his son,
As base, degenerate? 'By the eternal,' no!
While one sole arm remains to strike the blow!

[Cheers.]

I hail that hearty cheer — that stern reply;
"No! 'by the Eternal!' we prefer to die!"
You feel your sires' great spirits hov'ring near,
Who gaze intently on their sons' career;
Nay, all the ages which have passed away
Look down from Heaven upon our deeds this day,
To mark us worthy our illustrious sires;
Whose souls nor death, nor tribulation's fires,

Nor summer's heat, nor want, nor winter's cold,
Could e'er subdue.   And not alone the old,
But Nations yet unborn, and times remote,
Shall scan our record and our actions note,
To our eternal glory or our shame, ·
As worthy of the slave's or hero's name!

If in the humblest of our sires who died
For Liberty, we take an honest pride;
Our deeds this day to our posterity
The source of true nobility shall be!
Our children's children shall take pride to say,
' Our grandsires bled for liberty that day,
When cruel despots had in vain combined
The limbs of our young Liberty to bind!'

Then let us swear to die before we yield
One inch of ground, or quit the glorious field;
Their numbers will not shield the slaves from harm;
'T is Right alone that nerves the patriot's arm;

And conscious that their cause is base, unjust,
How can false traitors look to Heaven in trust?
Does any here for country fear to die?
Now is the time for such to turn and fly,
Nor act like thousands in a former fight,
Who turned their recreant backs in shameful flight,
And ran when none pursued. Should such again
Disgrace our country or its glory stain,
May God confound him! and may outraged Heaven
Blast his foul soul too black to be forgiven!
May blight fall on his field; rot on his flock;
And may his loved one's heart to him be rock;
Him may good men and matrons treat with scorn;
The youth and maidens shun — the urchins spurn;
Till loathing that vile life his fears would save,
He hopes, but hopes in vain, a coward's grave;
And torn by fell remorse — by men forgot,
He sinks to earth, and there is left to rot.
Or if remembered, let base infamy
Prey on his name in his posterity;
And let his race be cursed upon the earth;
Their homeless heads unblest by roof or hearth;

May they as outcasts through the world be driven,
Despised by men, disowned by God and Heaven!

.

But you who feel the patriot flame run high
And burn your bosoms, can you fear to die?
No, no! Your country calls; and you rejoice
To yield up all, obedient to her voice;
Oh, your reward shall be a glorious one;
The hero's death is endless life begun.

But should you live to see this flag unfurled,
The hope once more and glory of the world;
What joy and bliss await you in that hour,
When Freedom shall again assert her power;
And treason sink from its bad eminence:
Then shall the triumph of our race commence;
Then man redeemed, erect, shall walk abroad
On earth, and raise his grateful heart to God!
Now, soldiers, mark — By Him who rules on high,
I swear to conquer here, or here to die!"

And all respond — " By Him who rules on high,
We swear to conquer here, or here to die !"

And there they stand unmoved, a Godlike band,
Prepared to die, or save their Fatherland !
And let us pray, May they sustain the fight —
'T is God's own cause: May he defend the Right!

THE PRESIDENT'S WOOING.

MARCH, 1865

Our orb, once again, in her waltzing, hath run
Her annual course round her lover, the Sun;
And, friends, on this day, while I greet you again,
Let us hope the past year has not been spent in vain;
Let us hope that its record for ever will shine
In its own bright effulgence, a beacon divine,
To the Rulers and Peoples at home and abroad
Proclaiming that mercy is pleasing to God!
That a nation which free would remain, must be just,
And in God and his truth place their hope and their
    trust;
Turn away from the evil and tend more and more,
To virtue and light, and their great Source adore;
Till wrong in our world be for ever repressed,
And religion and charity rule in each breast;

Till, at length, our fair land, purged from slavery's
        dross,
Shall be chastened and meekly bow down at the
        cross;
Where all can exclaim, unrestricted and free,
"Behold, Lord, we offer true incense to thee,
The hearts of the noble, the gen'rous and brave,
Who have purged their loved soil of the despot and
        slave;
Those harpies, ill-omened, which never again
Shall pollute our Republic — its banner shall stain;
Whose croakings of virtue proclaim the death-knell,
And whose discord gives joy to the demons of hell!"

Ah! did we imagine we ever could build
A tower on such basis? or, that we could gild
Its rottenness so as to make it appear,
A fortress in danger — a refuge from fear?
If by such delusions our hearts have been held,
'Tis time such delusions from them were expelled;

For God, in his Word, hath proclaimed, that not
MIGHT

Could build up a nation, but VIRTUE and RIGHT!

But, what have we witnessed —? A people so blind,

As to worship all wealth, save the wealth of the
mind!

So that Israel was not so demented, by half,

When forgetful of God, he fell down to a calf.

Yes! Gold was our idol, our hope and our all,

And so we could clutch it, the Heavens might fall;

By this mighty Juggernaut nerves must be crushed,

While the cries and the groans of the tortured were
hushed;

As the Suttee's were drowned by the songs of the
priest,

Who averred that her bliss by her pangs was
increased;

And the vulgar were taught to believe that the pain

Of the martyr was pleasure, her torture was gain;

So we, every day, with indifference gazed
On the pile which with heaps of humanity blazed;
While the priests of the temple cried out: "Don't
    you see,
How blest their condition? They would not be free,
No, not if you offered them empires, as pay,
Would they make an exchange, so contented are they;
So joyous, so happy, so pleased with their state,
That to free them were madness — a tempting of
    fate!
What are nerves, what is muscle, what bruises and
    blood,
Compared with our gains? Merest foam on the flood!
Let nerves writhe in torture, blood flow in a tide,
Their sum serves to swell the vast stream of our
    pride!"
Thus, like those who partook of the lotus of old,
We were lulled in a trance — but our lotus was gold!

Then we saw splendid visions unfold to our eyes,
All earth as our empire, fenced round by the skies;

And all this domain a vast paradise spread
For those who had slaves to supply them in bread ;
Where each in abusing his slave should find bliss ;
And the bondsman should crave no more glory than
    this ;
To serve, to obey, and all torture endure,
If he for his master this joy could secure,
A sensual Paradise, crammed to excess
With all that gross nature can pamper or bless ;
And, happily, free from whatever might bind
The passions in chains, or enlighten the mind !

Such, such was our vision, our beautiful dream !
Ah ! why did it flee with the morning's first beam ?
Ah ! what was our horror, on waking, to view
Strange objects before us — a landscape quite new ;
Our Paradise swept by a plague, and replaced
By two armies in hostile array on a waste !
Before them was Plenty, but Ruin alone
Stalked behind, and claimed all they should leave as
    his own.

Thus the whirlwind we reap from our sowing the wind,
And a harvest of steel from the dragon's teeth find.

And hark to that sound! 't is the deafening peal
Of the cannon and musket, the clash of the steel!
War, Pestilence, Famine, appear on the stage,
Led on and incited by Fury and Rage;
• Peace flies in confusion, and earth is bereft
Of all hope, while a trace of the Dragon is left!

                              .

But Heaven unto mortals in mercy is kind,
And has scattered that seed, like the chaff by the
        wind;   .
And it never again shall take root in our soil,
To mock the slave's tortures and scoff at his toil.
Its doom was pronounced in the year that is passed,
And 't is hoped that the present will look on its last;
For though it was strong in its death agony;
The decree is gone forth—it is doomed—it must
        die!

Your Poet while soaring on Pegasus' wing,
Having prophesied thus, will descend and will sing
A song, (for he ever must something be doing,)
And that song shall be named — what?

THE PRESIDENT'S WOOING.

CHORUS —

>   The President has gone to woo;
>   Heigh, ho, the wooing o't!
>   Oh, say, what course will he pursue
>   To tame the wanton, wayward shrew?
>   (Not one alone, but all the crew;)
>   There's merit in the doing o't!

>   But hark! fair Columbia is wailing,
>   What sorrow has called forth her tears?
>   Are her sighs and her sobs unavailing,
>   To calm her forebodings and fears?

She gloomily sits there lamenting
 Her daughters, because "they are not,"
While their sisters are deeply repenting
 Those acts which cannot be forgot.

Hark! she calls " Carolina " — no answer!
 "Alabama and Georgia and all ;"
They are gone, as a prey to some cancer,
 Or frenzy — ! They heed not her call!

She counts o'er the stars on her banner,
 (The star-spangled banner of yore,)
One third are fallen off or grown wanner ;
 She knows it — she loves it no more !

She exclaims: " Can I trust to my senses?
 Have a few short years only passed by ;
Or have centuries worn our defenses,
 Or the sun gone astray in the sky ?

With Italy must we change places?
　Th' insulted and torn shall we be —
The 'Neobe, now, of the Nations,'
　While she is ' The home of the free?'

The Union, the Union is broken!
　Do I dream?　Alas, no!　Woe is me!
'T is too true! and this flag is a token;
　I lament for the Land of the Free!"

Wake up, fair Columbia, from sleeping;
　Your dream is sore troubled, no doubt;
For your daughters you 've vainly been weeping,
　They are not gone dead — just gone out!

They had heard of some change in the fashion,
　Or something gone wrong in that line;
No wonder they got in a passion,
　Concerning their loved crinoline!

18

And then, some unscrupulous fellows
　　Had told them their RIGHTS were assailed;
So the spirited damsels grew jealous,
　　And passion, not reason, prevailed.

And their lover long tried to persuade them
　　That their anger was kindled in vain;
" Their rights — he dreamt not to invade them,
　　Nor their honor to sully or stain!"

But they would not listen to reason,
　　Their fury could not be appeased;
So they rose in their might, (call it treason,)
　　And the PANTS they with violence seized;

And swore, in their wrath, they would wear them
　　Until all their wrongs were redressed;
But Abe, quite unwilling to spare them,
　　To regain them, now fawned and finessed.

But they would not yet yield to persuasion,
　　And so he tried gentle restraint,
Sought a trysting, (they called it invasion,)
　　Where each might prefer a complaint.

So they met him at Bull Run one morning,
　　And tugged pretty hard for the prize;
Gave Abe and his friends STRIKING warning,
　　By slapping them over the eyes!

And Abe now cried out in a passion,
　　"The jades scratch in earnest, that's flat!"
Commanded his henchmen to dash on,
　　And give them, right sharp, tit for tat!

So at Henry, at Donelson, Shiloh,
　　Port Arkansas, Champion Hill,
Port Gibson, Big Black, in grand style, oh!
　　He ground them like grist in the mill.

At Vicksburg, Pea-Ridge and Stone River,
　At Charleston, Richmond and all,
He caused them to shake and to shiver,
　And humbly for quarter to call.

And see, they are meekly returning;
　Their tresses gleam bright in the sun;
With blushes their fair cheeks are burning;
　They look like young brides wooed and won!

And lo! by their side yon bold suitor,
　The rail splitting youth; but, pray, hush!
No chap than Abe Lincoln is 'cuter,
　Their hearts he has mauled into mush!

And behold their bright eyes, how they glisten!
　Two stars some bring back, place of one;
Abe gabs, while they smile as they listen;
　The rail splitter's work is well done!

Hurrah for the Union, the Union!
   They 're " wooed and wedded and a' "
Henceforth we claim joyful communion,
   Hail friendship, love, liberty, law!

Chorus —

   The President has ceased to woo,
      Heigh, ho, the wooing o't!
      It boots not how he tamed the shrew,
      (Not one, but all the wayward crew;)
      Petruchio-like or Royal Jew —
   There's merit in the doing o't!

THE RETURN OF PEACE.

A SONNET.

*Zeffiro torna, e il bel tempo rimena.—*PETRARCH.

Now balmy Spring returns; and in her train
The Graces dance — the Hamadryads sing;
Gay Progne twitters softly 'midst the strain;
The robin and the bluebird prate of Spring;·
The clouds disperse — bright Heaven smiles again;
Jove glories in his daughter's faery wing;
Love holds o'er earth, sea, air, his happy reign;
All living creatures crown him for their king:
Then why should men alone be doomed to sigh?
The winter of our grief will soon be past;
We hail the gentle zephyrs floating by;
The storm of war has well-nigh blown its last:
Rebellion shattered never more shall rise;
Henceforth the cherub, Peace, shall gild our cloud-
  less skies!

TO MY DAUGHTER, FLORENCE,

ON HER BIRTHDAY, JANUARY 19.

The great Disposer, in his wise decree,
   Has fixed a time for all to live and die;
   And circumscribed, by vast eternity,
Our lives, as islands in a boundless sea.

Without our knowledge or consent we rose
   From out this wondrous night, we know not how;
   In weakness then — in bloom and vigor now,
But soon in gloom our brief career to close.

The space allotted is a changeful scene
   Of thought and feeling in life's theatre,
   Whereon to fret and fume a while; and here
Our acts are judged by critics stern and keen.

But, though the subjects of a just control,
 We are not, therefore, slaves of despot, Fate,
 To rule us with an iron hand elate;
We glory in the freedom of the soul!

Then, Florence, think, that as our actions are,
 So shall our hopes of future glory be;
 That soul alone is truly blest and free,
Whose guide on earth is virtue's polar star.

WORKS BY THE SAME AUTHOR.

OPINIONS OF THE PRESS:

THE TWO ANGELS, OR LOVE-LED. Price $1.00, Cloth.

From the *New Covenant:* "There is genuine poetry on every page, and whoever commences the perusal of 'The Two Angels,' will not lay the book down till he has finished it."

From the *Standard:* "Mr. Clarke's previous poems have all been well received by the press and the public. 'The Two Angels' is in advance of any of its predecessors. It takes captive the reader, and carries him away in spite of himself."

From the *Advance:* "'The Two Angels essays the great theme of the origin of evil. The plot posesses interest and power, while its influence is thrown upon the side of virtue and religion."

From the *Chicago Evening Journal:* "The story of 'The Two Angels' will bear witness to the learning and genius of its author."

SIR COPP: a Poem for the Times. Price $1.00, Cloth.

From the *Chicago Tribune;* "In this work we welcome another home-production. We must in justice commend this work for many striking and some admirable passages. The best English critics have accorded to Mr. Clarke a high rank among the first poets of the day."

From the *Chicago Evening Journal;* "Sir Copp is a poem in which patriotism of a high order, born of a right judgement of our late rebellion predominates; while poetry has not disdained to perch on the author's pen, and scatter telling satire, with here and there a bunch of flowers."

Sent free to any address, on receipt of the price. Agents who wish for profitable employment in selling these standard books, the best adapted for presentation of any ever published in the West, may apply for particulars and terms to

CLARKE & CO., PUBLISHERS,

170 Washington St.,
CHICAGO.

www.ingramcontent.com/pod-product-compliance
Lightning Source LLC
Chambersburg PA
CBHW030327270326
41926CB00010B/1537